Contents

To all the friends and family who it took to get this book out of my head and onto the page, proving that good things really are better when cooked up together.

Introduction

Welcome to Cook Together. This is not your ordinary cookbook. It's a unique culinary experience that aims to transform the way we cook, eat, and connect with one another. This collection of recipes has been carefully crafted for two individuals to start on a cooking journey together and makes the experience of sharing the kitchen as seamless as possible. My hope is that it will bring the health benefits of savouring your food, and the joys of being in the kitchen with someone you love, into perfect harmony.

As the costs of daily life go up, we increasingly find ourselves living in shared households. Yet loneliness and stress have fast become some of the most pressing issues of our time. How did we get here? One major factor is that we've become trapped by the convenience of our phones, the efficiency of meal delivery services, and the allure of collapsing onto the couch with reheated food, lost in the algorithms designed to isolate us. Although we live together more often, genuine connections around mealtimes seem to have slipped away.

Let's face it: After a long day at work, taking on the sole responsibility of preparing a meal often feels pretty daunting, especially when countless "easier" options are readily available. In the case of a couple, in the best-case scenario, the person with stronger culinary skills takes charge a few nights per week with the other picking up the slack every so often. However, traditional gender roles often take over and women are expected to tackle the cooking, or the burden falls disproportionately on whoever is home first, despite their equal, if not greater, workload.

Nutritionists may advocate for slow-cooked meals, whole foods, and homemade delicacies, but that all takes time, and these goals often take a backseat. This realization dawned on me during my work as a health coach; I saw so many smart young people struggling to prioritize time in the kitchen despite their awareness of the importance of nutrition and homecooked food.

Along with the temptation of apps and fast food, our cultural focus has shifted; we're at home less, we work longer hours, and, in many ways, the profound influence that cooking once held in our homes has been lost. This book seeks to restore cooking to its rightful place as a conduit for connection and nourishment.

Food possesses the remarkable power to bring people together, as exemplified by big holiday meals, potlucks, community barbecues, and even soup kitchens. These events create opportunities for people to gather, engage in conversation, indulge in nourishing food, and enjoy the company of their community. The common thread that unites them all? The shared responsibility of cooking. The joy lies in the fact that no one person bears the burden alone. We get so much pleasure from trying a variety of dishes prepared by different hands: Uncle Cassidy's BBQ brisket alongside Auntie Alice's favourite potato salad. Dad expertly pouring drinks, and Cousin Mia proudly presenting her famous hummus. The collaborative spirit is what makes those meals truly special.

Consider the contrast between a typical dinner party and a potluck gathering. While dinner parties have their charm, they place an overwhelming burden on the host. As a chef and frequent host myself, I understand the feeling all too well. Hours spent preparing food, occasional frustrations directed at my partner or kids, and exhaustion masked by forced smiles when guests arrive. The lesson is clear: Given the choice between a dinner party and a potluck where everyone shares the load, the latter wins, hands down. Cook Together is the potluck to traditional cookbooks' dinner parties.

Introduction

But beyond the enjoyment of cooking side by side, Cook Together has a deeper purpose. By embracing the experience of cooking together, you'll not only strengthen your relationship but also rediscover the art of savouring food slowly and deliberately. In a world that often rushes through meals, this book invites you to slow down, engage all your senses, and truly appreciate the culinary delights and the company that grace your table. Each recipe has been crafted to foster socialization and intimacy, encouraging you and your partner to dive into the act of preparing dinner together and creating not just meals, but lasting memories.

The final piece of the Cook Together mission is nutrition. In compiling these 30 recipes, I've picked a mix of my favourite dishes and comfort foods from around the world. I've either stayed true to their healthy roots or modified them to be a more nutritious version of that dish. My goal is that if you only cooked the recipes in this book, you would have a great balanced diet.

What you won't find here: ultra-processed foods, unnecessary added sugar, added chemicals, or cooking techniques that strip essential nutrients. What you will find: hearty food for all seasons, new and exciting global ingredients that tease your senses, and most importantly, food that leaves you full and satisfied until your next meal.

At the heart of Cook Together lies a belief in the nourishing power of shared meals. As you join forces in the kitchen, you'll engage in meaningful conversations, creating space for connection and understanding. With every bite, you'll savour not only the flavours but also the laughter, the stories, and the intimate moments that make your relationship unique.

Welcome to Cook Together, a cookbook that goes beyond the ordinary, guiding you on a transformative journey of preparing food for pleasure and above all else, togetherness.

How it works

Let's reflect on the restaurant experience. Complex and impressive dishes are prepared and presented to you with remarkable speed. From the moment you place your order, it often takes no more than 20 minutes for the food to grace your table. So, how are they so quick? Well, there's a team of individuals working behind that kitchen door. Even small establishments have prep cooks and line cooks. **The prep cooks meticulously handle all the ingredients, getting everything ready for the line cooks to transform into mouth-watering dishes**. This restaurant model forms the foundation of Cook Together – the belief that many hands make light work, inspired by those places where efficiency is paramount, and there's no compromise on quality.

You've probably never seen a recipe written for two people before. I hadn't either, which is why I've written this book. Given that it's a first for all of us, there are a few things we should discuss.

YOU, ME, US.

I've written each recipe with two clear roles. YOU is one person. ME is the other. While the recipes may vary in terms of techniques and ingredients, there are certain things I've kept consistent.

YOU is typically written as a line cook role, while ME is more of a prep chef. ME is going to take the lead on chopping vegetables, measuring ingredients for sauces, and generally (but not always) handing these things off to YOU to cook. YOU is going to be the person who cooks the ingredients that ME has prepped. That could mean getting a frying pan to caramelize the cut onions, or creating a vegetable broth from ME's trimmings.

My recommendation is to begin with the roles that you both feel most comfortable in. If one of you is more comfortable with a sharp knife and a chopping board, they should be ME. If one of you is confident with cooking meat or vegetables, make them YOU. If there is no obvious split, then just pick one. These recipes are straightforward and simple. Neither person will fail in either role.

...And on the next recipe, maybe swap. You might find that one person just generally likes one role better long term. That's great. If not, flip-flop for the next meal. However, it is important to maintain consistency within each recipe, sticking to the assigned roles until your meal is ready.

And finally, as you each complete the tasks assigned to YOU and ME, you will see a section called US. This is where the roles come together to finish off the dish with teamwork. On some dishes, this is as simple as combining the elements you have been preparing. On others, you'll work together to finish cooking the pièce de résistance. Usually these are recipes where four hands are better than two for the final steps.

You'll see that at the back of this book (starting on page 171) I've also included each recipe written in the traditional style for one person to complete. I'd like you to be able to fall in love with a dish you've made with a friend and be able to make it alone if the mood strikes.

Timings

I've structured each task list for YOU and ME, with the idea that they will come together in about the same amount of time. Most of these recipes are designed to take approximately 30 minutes with two focused cooks. However, it's difficult to estimate the speed of your knife skills or how distracted your partner might get from what they are doing. Therefore, I recommend approaching each recipe with a relaxed energy, and not get caught up in who can do what fastest.

If YOU find yourself waiting a few extra minutes for ME to finish chopping mushrooms, that's perfectly fine. Simply keep an eye on the pan and remove it from the stove if it starts to get too hot while you wait. None of these recipes will turn into a disaster if something is three minutes behind schedule.

For those recipes that take a little longer, or if you find yourself with nothing to do while your partner completes a task or while a dish simmers, take the opportunity to start cleaning up. There's a certain satisfaction in finishing the cooking process and having a clean space to enjoy your meal!

Here are a few suggestions for how to utilize any spare moments during the recipe, whether you're alone or together:

- Get DJing. A great playlist can make the whole process more fun and set a nice pace for the recipe.
- Make and serve drinks. I usually like a cold drink in the kitchen because of the heat from the equipment, but a hot drink like tea or coffee works great, too.
- Have conversation! I've included a list of fun conversation topics and ice breakers to help get you started in the back of the book (page 209). You can start with those or just catch up on your day. I've found that some of the best conversations happen when our hands or feet are occupied with another task. Sometimes it's harder to talk openly if you're making too much eye contact, so cooking is a great way to catch up.

Stations and Set-up

This is an important subject, and it's the catch that makes cooking together possible – even in the smallest spaces. Give yourself what we call in the cooking industry a "station." This enables smooth collaboration and ensures everyone has their own functional area. Prepare a small, clean surface that extends slightly beyond your shoulder width to serve as a dedicated space where you can comfortably manoeuvre. I like to set up my station ahead of cooking the recipe, so I know I have everything I need.

If you assume the role of ME, you'll likely require a chopping board, a knife, and a few bowls to hold prepped ingredients. As for YOU, secure some bowls and counter space, ideally next to the stove or hob. Consider sharing measuring cups, scales, or bowls between you or having separate sets available. I cannot stress enough the importance of having enough bowls or containers when cooking with a partner. These offer easy organization, cleanliness, and allow for passing of ingredients between you. Personally, I often use Tupperware and metal mixing bowls, but depending on the recipe, having a few measuring jugs on hand can be helpful as well.

Make sure your station is not on top of your partner's. You don't want to be bumping shoulders for the whole recipe. I've seen these recipes successfully executed in tiny boat galleys, so your kitchen is likely big enough for two well prepared stations.

If your partner is not used to cooking in your kitchen, spend five minutes before you start to familiarize them with the location of everything. This will pre-empt a barrage of questions once you're underway. Additionally, I recommend taking five minutes to gather and arrange all the ingredients for the recipe beforehand. This way you can both easily fetch what you need, as you need it.

By setting up organized stations and ensuring a smooth start, you can maximize efficiency and enjoyment while cooking together.

Communication

Just like any collaborative activity, effective communication is crucial when cooking together. Communication is mostly through words (although Gordon Ramsay might prefer shouting and swearing), but non-verbal cues such as eye contact, nods, or gentle nudges can also play a role.

These are the three key areas of communication in the kitchen:

1. Ensuring your partner is ok with timings: It's important to check in as the recipe progresses to make sure everything's on track. It can be frustrating if you rush through your portion only to discover that your partner has been engrossed in social media for the past ten minutes.

2. Understanding each other's taste preferences: Take into consideration each other's taste preferences and any dietary restrictions or allergies. How spicy do you like your food? Does cilantro/coriander taste like soap to you? If so, leave it out.

3. Communicating your location in the kitchen: Sometimes there's no time for "please" and "thank you" in the kitchen. Short sharp communication is the order of the day – particularly if you're carrying a knife or hot pan. Here are some quick, fun phrases to help you talk like a chef, feel like a chef, and inject some team spirit into your kitchen:

"Hot behind"/"sharp behind" – When you move a hazardous object in a small space, you should make it known.

"In the weeds" – This is a fun way of saying that you're getting behind and might need some help.

"Fire" – Rather than indicating that something is ablaze, this lets your fellow chef know they can go ahead with their cooking. As in, "fire the chicken."

"Heard that" – This indicates that you have heard what your co-chef is asking. It's a great way to acknowledge them and keep things moving.

By integrating these communication strategies and injecting some chef-like phrases into your cooking, you can enhance teamwork, efficiency, and overall enjoyment while cooking together.

Serving Sizes

All the recipes in this book are written to serve two hungry people. You may find that you have leftovers some days and not others, depending on how big certain ingredients are the day you're cooking, e.g., one butternut squash is not always the same size as another. If you are cooking these recipes for a group, be sure to increase the quantities accordingly.

Cooking Techniques

I cover a lot of basic techniques in this book, but I'll go through a few here so there's no confusion over language I use.

1. Sauté: Quickly cook food in a small amount of fat over high heat, while stirring or tossing frequently. It's a method that allows for fast cooking and browning.

2. Sear: Cook food over high heat until the surface is browned, sealing in juices and creating a flavourful crust. Searing is commonly used for meats and seafood to enhance flavour and texture.

3. Fry: Cook food submerged in hot oil or fat, typically in a pan or deep fryer. Frying results in a crispy exterior.

4. Simmer: Gently cook food in liquid just below boiling, with small bubbles breaking the surface. This method is ideal for slow and gentle cooking, allowing flavours to meld together.

5. Boil: Cook food in liquid at a high temperature where large bubbles constantly rise and break the surface. This method is commonly used for cooking pasta, vegetables, and other ingredients that require a more vigorous cooking process.

6. Blanch: Briefly cook food in boiling water, then transfer it to ice water to halt the cooking process. Blanching is often used to partially cook vegetables before further preparation, such as freezing or sautéing.

7. Roast: Cook food, typically meat or vegetables, in an oven at a high temperature. This method results in a browned exterior and tender interior, creating delicious flavours and textures.

8. Grill: Cook food under direct heat, often in an oven, resulting in browning and caramelization. This method is great for quickly cooking or adding a golden crust to dishes. UK version of Broil.

9. Broil: Cook food under direct heat, often in an oven, resulting in browning and caramelization. This method is great for quickly cooking or adding a golden crust to dishes. American version of Grill.

Cooking Techniques

10. Bake: Cook food in an oven, surrounded by dry heat. Baking is commonly used for cakes, bread, pastries, and other baked goods, resulting in a tender and flavorful outcome.

11. Steam: Cook food by suspending it over boiling water in a covered pot, allowing the steam to cook the food. Steaming preserves nutrients and produces moist and delicate results.

12. Poach: Cook food gently in liquid below boiling temperature. Poaching is suitable for delicate items like eggs or fish, providing a tender and moist outcome.

13. Grate: Shred food into small, fine pieces using a grater. This technique is often used for cheese, vegetables, or citrus zest to incorporate into dishes.

14. Marinate: Soak food, usually meat or vegetables, in a mixture of liquids and seasonings to enhance flavour and tenderness. Marinating adds depth and complexity to the final dish.

15. Fold: Gently combine ingredients by using a spatula to cut vertically through the mixture and bring the bottom to the top. Folding is often used in delicate recipes to preserve airiness.

16. Reduce: Simmer a liquid, allowing it to evaporate and thicken, intensifying flavours. Reducing is often used to concentrate sauces and enhance their richness.

17. Zest: Remove the outer colored portion of citrus fruit peel, often using a grater, to add flavour and aroma to dishes. Zest is packed with essential oils and adds brightness and tang.

18. Dice: Cut food into small, even cubes, usually around ¼ inch in size. This technique ensures uniformity in shape and size.

19. Mince: Finely chop food into tiny, uniform pieces. Mincing creates small, almost paste-like texture for ingredients.

20. Chop: Cut food into small, irregular pieces. The size of the chop can vary depending on the recipe or personal preference, allowing for versatility in texture.

21. Slice: Cut food into flat, thin pieces with consistent thickness. Slicing is commonly used for creating uniform layers or pieces of ingredients.

American English vs. UK English

I grew up in the US with an American dad and an English mom. At the time of writing this book I've been living in London for 7 years. I've worked with food as a private chef and a nutritionist in both countries, so as you can imagine, it was hard to pick a format for this book. As you may know, many of the words differ between American and UK English, particularly around food. I don't want to exclude anyone so I've decided to incorporate both terms where possible but I wanted to include a glossary of terms used in this book so you can double check if you get confused.

UK	USA
Beetroot	Beets
Chips	Fries
Cling film	Plastic wrap
Coriander	Cilantro
Grill	Broiler
Heritage	Heirloom
Hob	Stove
Kichen roll	Paper Towel
Pak choi	Bok choi
Prawn	Shrimp
Spring onion	Scallion
Tin	Can

The Recipes

This book is comprised of meals that are, above all, delicious, healthy, and fun. I've had the good fortune to live in many major cities both in the US and the UK, and to travel extensively. Along the way, I've been exposed to some of the most incredible cuisine the world has to offer. These dishes have inspired many of these recipes, which don't represent my personal heritage or traditions. While I've tried to retain many of the elements that make those dishes special, I've modified them to include ingredients that are easy to access, and these recipes are very much my variations.

Equipment

There are some pieces of basic kitchen equipment I think everyone should have (and they come up throughout this book):

1. Sharp knives in at least two sizes – A chef's knife and a paring knife are the most useful. It's essential to keep your knives sharp. This is a lifelong investment.

2. Chopping boards.

3. Mixing bowls (various sizes).

4. Measuring cups and spoons.

5. Wooden spoon, whisk, spatula, tongs, peeler.

6. Colander – A colander is a bowl-shaped kitchen tool with small holes that allow liquid to drain out while keeping solid ingredients contained.

7. Graters in different sizes for zesting citrus or grating cheese.

8. Baking sheets: A baking sheet, also known as a baking tray or cookie sheet, is a flat metal sheet with raised edges.

9. Saucepans (large, medium, and small): Saucepans are deep, straight-sided pots with a long handle and a lid.

10. Ovenproof skillet or frying pans (such as cast-iron) – These pans have a flat bottom and low sides, allowing for easy flipping and tossing of ingredients. They are designed to be used on stovetops for frying, sautéing, and searing, and are safe to go in the oven, making them suitable for dishes that require finishing in the oven. Cast-iron skillets are known for their excellent heat retention and distribution.

11. Nonstick skillet or frying pans – These pans have a special coating that prevents food from sticking to the surface. Be sure to buy one that is non-toxic.

12. Blender: A blender is used for blending and pureeing ingredients. Ideal for soups, sauces, and other liquid-based recipes.

13. Food processor – A food processor is used for chopping, slicing, grating, pureeing, and mixing ingredients.

Hopefully now you feel empowered to get into the kitchen as you work together. So, grab your aprons and utensils, and embrace the joy of creating delicious meals that will nourish you both. May your kitchen be filled with laughter, experimentation, and the satisfaction of a job well done.

Happy cooking!

Chapter One:

Hearty Vegetarian

Lentil Dhal with Speedy Dosa

I remember the first time I was served a dhal. It was at a friend's house for lunch. She was going through a vegan phase, which lasted about a week, but I was immediately in love. The way that dhal balances immense flavor while also being a soothing comfort food is unlike any other dish. Indian spices bring so much life to pantry ingredients, and in this dhal, the ginger and turmeric paired with coconut milk and lentils creates something that would soothe even the grumpiest of moods. My quick buckwheat dosas add some nice texture. Make sure you use a hot pan to cook them. I like to serve this dhal with a dollop of yogurt on top.

See recipe for one in the kitchen on page 171

For the Dhal:

1 medium tomato

1 small bunch of fresh cilantro/coriander (about 1 cup)

3 garlic cloves

1 thumb-size piece of fresh ginger

1 tablespoon olive oil

1 small red onion

1 to 2 red chilis (depending on your heat preference)

5 dried curry leaves

1 teaspoon ground turmeric

½ teaspoon ground cumin

½ teaspoon fenugreek seeds

One 14-ounce (400 g) can full-fat coconut milk

¾ cup (150 g) red split lentils

¼ teaspoon salt

For the Dosas:

1 large egg

½ cup plus 1 tablespoon (150 ml) milk

¾ cup (100 g) buckwheat flour

1 tablespoon melted unsalted butter

¼ teaspoon sea or kosher salt

Olive oil

For Serving:

½ cup plain yogurt (you can also use coconut yogurt), for serving

Ingredients

You

1 medium tomato

1 small bunch of fresh cilantro/coriander (about 1 cup)

3 garlic cloves

1 thumb-size piece of fresh ginger

1 tablespoon olive oil

5 dried curry leaves

1 teaspoon ground turmeric

½ teaspoon ground cumin

½ teaspoon fenugreek seeds

One 14-ounce (400 g) can full-fat coconut milk

¾ cup (150 g) red split lentils

¼ teaspoon salt

1. Make the dhal: In a food processor or blender, place the tomato, ¾ cup of the coriander (including the stems), the garlic, and ginger with ¼ cup (60 ml) water. Blend and set aside.

2. In a large pot over medium heat, heat the olive oil and add the onion and chilis. Cook until translucent, 5 to 7 minutes.

3. Add the curry leaves, turmeric, cumin, and fenugreek seeds and cook for 1 minute more.

4. Add the blended tomato mixture and turn the heat up slightly. Reduce until the liquid is absorbed.

5. Add the coconut milk, lentils, salt, and ¾ cup (175 ml) water. Bring to a boil. Put a lid on and reduce to a simmer, stirring regularly, until the lentils are soft, about 20 minutes.

Ingredients

1 small red onion, thinly sliced

1 to 2 red chilis (depending on personal taste), thinly sliced

1 large egg, beaten

½ cup plus 1 tablespoon (150 ml) milk

¾ cup (100 g) buckwheat flour

1 tablespoon melted unsalted butter

¼ teaspoon sea or kosher salt

Olive oil

Me

1. Peel and thinly slice the onion. Chop the chilis. Pass these to YOU

2. Make the dosas: In a bowl, add the egg, milk, 1/2 cup plus 1 tablespoon (150 ml) water, the buckwheat flour, butter, and salt to make a batter that's like a crepe batter, i.e., slightly runnier than a regular pancake batter. Add more water if needed.

3. Heat a nonstick skillet or crepe pan over high heat. Wait until the pan is very hot and add a little bit of oil. Ladle a scoop of the batter into the pan. Use the handle of the pan to swirl the batter around the pan into a thin layer. It should start to bubble immediately.

4. Drizzle 1 teaspoon olive oil around the edge of each dosa so it crisps up.

5. When the bottom turns dark gold-brown and the edges are crispy, flip the dosa over. Cook another 30 seconds and transfer to a plate.

6. Repeat with the rest of the batter to make more dosas.

Us

½ cup plain yogurt (you can also use coconut yogurt), for serving

1. Ladle the dhal curry into two bowls, top with a spoonful of yogurt, and serve with the dosas on the side.

Sweet Potato and Cabbage Pad Thai

Some of the best recipes come when I need to use up ingredients in the fridge. This recipe is no exception, but it quickly became a household favorite. If you're a fan of pad Thai but want to switch things up and add some healthy veggies to the mix, you're in for a treat. This is the perfect fusion of classic Thai flavors and nutritious ingredients. The combination of sweet potato and cabbage to replace the traditional noodles adds a delicious crunch to the dish, while the traditional pad Thai sauce brings a balance of salty, sour, and sweet flavors. If you want more protein, you can top this with fish or chicken, but we love it just as it is!

See recipe for one in the kitchen on page 172

For the Sauce:

2 tablespoons tamari or soy sauce

2 tablespoons peanut butter or almond butter

2 limes

1 tablespoon sesame oil

1 teaspoon honey

1 teaspoon sriracha

1-inch piece of fresh ginger

2 garlic cloves

For the Pad Thai:

¼ cup vegetable oil

1 garlic clove

2 chilis

½ cup raw, lightly salted cashews

2 medium sweet potatoes

1 small or ½ medium white cabbage

2 scallions or spring onions

Ingredients

You

2 tablespoons tamari or soy sauce

2 tablespoons peanut butter or
almond butter

1 tablespoon sesame oil

1 teaspoon honey

1 teaspoon sriracha

1/4 cup vegetable oil

1. Juice 3 lime halves from ME.

2. Combine the tamari, almond butter, lime juice, sesame oil, honey, and sriracha to make the sauce.

3. Add the grated ginger and garlic from ME to the sauce.

4. Line a plate with a paper towel.

5. Heat the vegetable oil in a small saucepan over medium heat and add the sliced garlic from ME. Fry until bubbles just stop appearing but before the garlic changes color, about 2 minutes. Use a slotted spoon to transfer to the prepared plate.

6. Add the sliced chilis to this same oil and fry for another minute, until the small bubbles stop appearing. Remove with a slotted spoon and reserve the oil.

7. Heat 1 tablespoon of the chili-garlic oil in a large frying pan over medium-high heat and add the sweet potato. Cook for 5 minutes and add the cabbage and 1/4 cup water. Cook until the sweet potato is soft and the cabbage is wilted but hasn't lost its color, another 5 minutes.

Ingredients

2 limes

1-inch piece of fresh ginger

3 garlic cloves

2 chilis

2 medium sweet potatoes

1 small or ½ medium white cabbage

2 scallions or spring onions

½ cup raw, lightly salted cashews

Me

1. Halve the limes and cut one half into segments. Hand these to YOU.

2. Grate the ginger and 2 garlic cloves. Hand these to YOU.

3. Thinly slice the chilis and remaining 1 garlic clove. Hand these to YOU.

4. Peel the sweet potato and grate it on a thick grater.

5. Slice the cabbage in half and then slice down each half thinly to create "noodles."

6. Thinly slice 2 scallions.

7. In a small pan over medium heat, add the cashews. Toast for 5 minutes. Remove from the heat and coarsely chop them.

Us

1. Toss the cooked cabbage and sweet potato with the sauce and garnish with the scallions, cashews, fried chilis, and fried garlic. Serve with lime wedges on the side.

Socca Bread with Paneer Salad

Socca Bread with Paneer Salad

If, like me, you are obsessed with Indian cuisine and are simultaneously looking for gluten-free bread alternatives, then this Socca bread is going to change your life. Even if you have just a normal level of excitement about Indian cuisine, you also won't be disappointed! Hailing from the southern region of France, Socca bread is traditionally made with chickpea flour and water, then baked until it's crispy and savoury. This recipe takes it to the next level by incorporating bold and aromatic spices commonly used in Indian cooking: turmeric, cumin, coriander, cardamom. The resulting crisp bread is garnished with the ultimate grilled Indian fresh cheese, paneer. If you can't find paneer, feel free to substitute halloumi, but remember to skip adding the salt, as halloumi is already quite salty.

See recipe for one in the kitchen on page 173

For the Socca:

½ cup (75 g) chickpea flour

3 tablespoons olive oil

1 teaspoon ground turmeric

1 teaspoon salt

½ teaspoon ground cumin

3 cardamom pods

1 teaspoon coriander seeds

1 red onion

2 garlic cloves

For the Salad:

2 handfuls (100 g) of baby spinach

½ red onion

For the Paneer:

3 ½ ounces (100 g) paneer

1 handful of peanuts

¼ teaspoon cayenne pepper

½ teaspoon salt

1 to 2 tablespoons olive oil

For the Dressing:

1 tablespoon honey

Juice of ½ lemon

2 tablespoons olive oil

½ teaspoon salt

½ teaspoon cayenne pepper

Ingredients

½ cup (75 g) chickpea flour

5 tablespoons olive oil

1 teaspoon ground turmeric

½ teaspoon ground cumin

1 1/2 teaspoons salt

1 red onion

2 garlic cloves

3 cardamom pods (see Note)

1 teaspoon coriander seeds

1 tablespoon honey

Juice of ½ lemon

½ teaspoon cayenne pepper

Note: You can crush cardamom pods in a mortar and pestle or use the back of a knife to gently crack them open, revealing their flavorful seeds.

You

1. Preheat the oven to the Broil/Grill setting at 450°F (230°C).

2. In a medium bowl, add the chickpea flour, ½ cup (120 ml) water, 1 tablespoon of olive oil, the turmeric, 1 teaspoon of salt, and the cumin. Mix thoroughly and set aside for 15 minutes.

3. In a small bowl, whisk together the honey, lemon juice, 2 tablespoons of olive oil, the remaining ½ teaspoon salt, and the cayenne pepper.

4. In a cast-iron (or any ovenproof) pan over medium heat, add the crushed cardamom pods, making sure to release the seeds, and the coriander seeds. Toast for 30 seconds before adding the remaining 2 tablespoons olive oil and the sliced onion from ME. Sweat the onion until it starts to brown, 5 minutes. Add the chopped garlic from ME and cook for 1 to 2 more minutes.

5. Remove the cardamom shells.

6. Pour the batter into the hot pan and transfer the mixture to cook under the hot broiler/grill for 12 minutes.

Ingredients

1 red onion

2 garlic cloves

2 handfuls (100 g) of baby spinach

3 ½ ounces (100 g) paneer

1 to 2 tablespoons olive oil

¼ teaspoon cayenne pepper

½ teaspoon salt

1 handful of peanuts

Me

1. Thinly slice the onion and pass half to YOU. Finely chop the rest for the salad and set aside.

2. Slice 2 garlic cloves and pass to YOU.

3. Wash and dry the baby spinach and roughly chop the leaves.

4. Line a plate with paper towels and set aside.

5. Dice the paneer into 1-centimeter cubes and in a bowl mix with peanuts, cayenne pepper, and salt.

6. In a nonstick pan over medium-high heat, heat the olive oil. Add the paneer-peanut mixture and fry until both are lightly browned, 2 to 3 minutes.

7. Remove and transfer to the prepared plate.

Us

1. Make the salad: In a medium bowl, toss together the spinach, red onion, peanuts, and paneer. Lightly coat with the dressing.

2. Remove the socca bread from the oven. Let it cool slightly. Slice into quarters and top with the fresh salad.

Tapas-Style Tortilla with Confit Peppers

Tapas-Style Tortilla with Confit Peppers

This classic Spanish tapas dish is also known commonly as a Spanish omelette. The traditional way of making this is to deep fry the potatoes before adding them to the egg mixture but by roasting them here you save a lot of mess. The confit peppers and garlic are one of my favorite things to have on hand in the house and the infused olive oil that is a by-product is a great thing to keep in the cupboard for salad dressings or frying eggs!

See recipe for one in the kitchen on page 174

Ingredients

1 pound (450 g) new potatoes

1 cup plus 1 tablespoon (250 ml) olive oil

1 large or 2 small bell peppers

2 garlic cloves

A few sprigs of fresh thyme

1 yellow onion

8 large eggs

Salt and freshly ground black pepper

4 good medium tomatoes or 2 large heritage/heirloom tomatoes

1 tablespoon balsamic vinegar

Small chunk of Manchego cheese

Ingredients

You

1 cup plus 1 tablespoon (250 ml) olive oil

A few sprigs of fresh thyme

2 garlic cloves

1. Preheat the oven to 410°F (210°C).

2. On a baking sheet, toss the sliced potatoes from ME with 1 tablespoon of the olive oil. Bake for 15 to 18 minutes, until beginning to brown and cook through.

3. Measure the remaining 1 cup (230 ml) olive oil into a small saucepan and heat over medium-low heat. Add the sliced bell peppers from ME. You don't want it to start smoking or boiling, just a low simmer. Add the thyme and garlic.

4. Cook slowly. If the bell peppers aren't covered by the oil, use the back of a spoon to press them down gently every 5 minutes until they do. Cook submerged in the oil for 20 to 30 minutes, or until you are ready to serve.

5. Add 1 tablespoon of the olive oil spooned off the top of the bell peppers to a 10-inch nonstick skillet and add the sliced onions from ME. Fry in the oil for 15 minutes until beginning to brown all over. Remove from the heat. Don't clean the pan, just set it aside.

Ingredients

Me

1 pound (450 g) new potatoes

1 large or two small bell peppers

1 yellow onion

8 large eggs

Salt and freshly ground black pepper

4 good medium tomatoes or 2 large heritage/

heirloom tomatoes

1 tablespoon balsamic vinegar

1. Thinly slice the potatoes. Pass these to YOU.

2. Remove the stem and seeds from the bell peppers and thinly slice them. Pass these to YOU.

3. Peel, halve, and thinly slice the onion.

4. Crack the eggs into a bowl, add 1 teaspoon salt, and whisk together.

5. Cut the tomatoes into wedges and toss with the balsamic vinegar and some salt and pepper. Allow to marinate until ready to serve.

See next page for us directions.

Ingredients

Us

8 large eggs

Small chunk of Manchego cheese (optional)

1. Preheat the oven to the Broil/Grill setting at 450°F (230°C).

2. While whisking, slowly drizzle 2 tablespoons of the hot oil from the bell peppers into the prepared eggs from ME. This will prevent the oil from cooking the eggs.

3. Combine the eggs with the cooked potatoes and caramelized onions in the same bowl.

4. Pour this mixture back into the pan you caramelized the onion with. Place over medium heat. After about 6 minutes, the tortilla should be set around the edge with a slightly runny middle.

5. Transfer the tortilla into the oven and broil for 4 minutes. Remove and allow to cool.

6. Grate the Manchego (if using) over the top of the balsamic tomatoes.

7. Drain the peppers and season with salt. Save the olive oil from them for another use!

8. Slice the tortilla into wedges and serve with the bell peppers and the balsamic tomatoes on the side.

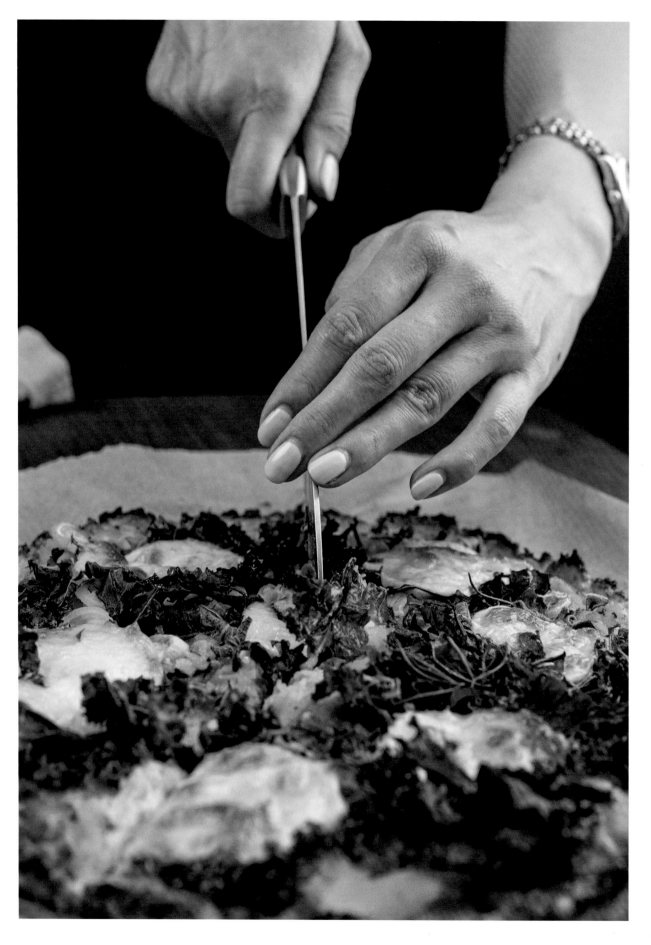

Cauliflower Pizza with Sage and Butternut Squash

I've been stuck on the cauliflower pizza train since it first surfaced mid-Paleo craze in the early 2010s. Cauliflower is a super versatile ingredient. As a pizza crust, it's got great flavor, texture, and feels pretty guilt-free. But it's a pain to make alone. The steaming, the squeezing, the baking—it's not hard work, but it takes a while, which is why it's the perfect recipe to cook together. With two of you working alongside each other, this will come together so quickly and easily. Make sure you squeeze as much water out of the steamed cauliflower as possible, so your dough holds together. This recipe is slightly different from the others in this book, as you will make the crust together and then work on the toppings after you've got it in the oven.

See recipe for one in the kitchen on page 175

For the Crust:

1 small to medium head of cauliflower

1 large egg

½ cup (120 g) soft goat cheese

Salt and freshly ground black pepper

For the Toppings:

½ butternut squash

1 ½ tablespoons olive oil

2 garlic cloves

1 cup (100 g) curly kale

4 ounces (100 g) fresh mozzarella cheese

1 large shallot

About 10 leaves of fresh sage

About 2 sprigs of fresh rosemary

Ingredients

1 large egg

½ cup (120 g) soft goat cheese

Salt and freshly ground black pepper

½ butternut squash

1 tablespoon olive oil

2 garlic cloves

You

1.   Preheat the oven to 400F (200C). Line 2 large baking sheets with parchment paper.

2.   In a medium bowl, combine the egg, goat cheese, and a pinch each of salt and pepper.

3.   Peel the skin from the squash, remove the seeds and any stringy bits and cut into small pieces. On one of the prepared baking sheets, add the squash and toss with the olive oil and garlic. Set aside.

Ingredients

1 small to medium head of cauliflower

4 ounces (100 g) fresh mozzarella cheese

2 sprigs of fresh rosemary

1 large shallot

About 10 leaves of fresh sage

1 cup (100 g) curly kale

½ tablespoon olive oil

Me

1. Cut the florets from the cauliflower stem and place in a blender or food processor and blend until you get a rice-like consistency.

2. Bring a large pot of water to a boil.

3. Add the ground florets to the boiling water and reduce to simmer for 1 minute.

4. Drain in a fine-mesh sieve, pressing to get the water out. Set aside to cool.

Us

1. Working together in batches, squeeze the cauliflower in 2 clean dish towels. Each batch should be no larger than a tennis ball. Squeeze to drain out as much liquid as possible. The more you squeeze, the better your crust will hold together.

2. Add the drained cauliflower to the bowl with the egg and goat cheese mixture and combine to form a wet dough.

3. On the second prepared baking sheet, spread this dough into a round shape and use your hands to press it about 1/8-inch-thick with a slightly raised rim.

4. Bake the crust for 40 to 45 minutes until lightly toasted in color. Remove and allow to cool slightly.

5. At the same time the crust bakes, roast the squash for about 30 minutes, until soft.

6. Keep the oven on.

See next page for more directions

You

1. Mash the squash into a paste.

Me

1. Slice the mozzarella into 1/4-inch-thick rounds.

2. Thinly slice the shallot.

3. Roughly chop the sage and rosemary.

4. Remove the stem from the kale and cut into bite-size pieces. Massage with the olive oil.

Us

1. Spread the mashed butternut squash over the crust.

2. Add the mozzarella, kale, shallot, sage, and rosemary and bake for another 10 minutes, or until the cheese is melted.

Cauliflower Pizza with Sage and Butterut Squash

Giant Black Bean Burger with Sweet Potato Fries

Giant Black Bean Burger with Sweet Potato Fries

This veggie burger will satisfy junk food cravings but leave you feeling clean and light. The caramelized pepper and onion are essential in giving this burger some of that savoury umami that is hard to find in bean burgers. I usually make this recipe into two BIG burgers – because no one wants a tiny veggie burger – but you can make it into three average-size ones and have a spare if you so desire. Either way, you're going to need a few napkins on hand while you eat these messy numbers. Don't skimp on the sweet potato fries, either. I like to cut them nice and skinny, so they crisp up in the oven.

See recipe for one in the kitchen on page 176

For the Patties:

½ bell pepper

½ small yellow onion

2 garlic cloves

One 14-ounce (400 g) can black beans

2 large eggs

2 tablespoons tomato paste

1 teaspoon ground cumin

1 teaspoon salt

½ teaspoon garlic powder

½ teaspoon smoked paprika

¼ cup (30 g) breadcrumbs

Unsalted butter

2 burger buns

3 tablespoons olive oil

2 slices sharp/mature cheddar cheese

1 head of baby gem lettuce

1 avocado

For the Fries:

2 small sweet potatoes, or 1 large

2 tablespoons olive oil

1 teaspoon salt

Ingredients

You

One 14-ounce (400 g) can black beans

2 large eggs

2 tablespoons tomato paste

1 teaspoon ground cumin

1 teaspoon salt

½ teaspoon garlic powder

½ teaspoon smoked paprika

1 tablespoon olive oil

¼ cup (30 g) breadcrumbs

1. In a large bowl, combine the beans, eggs, tomato paste, cumin, garlic powder, salt, and paprika. Mash together with a fork or potato masher to break up the beans. Set aside.

2. In a medium skillet over medium heat, heat the olive oil and add the chopped vegetables from ME. Cook until translucent and starting to caramelize, 10 minutes. Allow to cool slightly.

3. Add the vegetables and the breadcrumbs to the bean mixture, thoroughly combining.

4. Form the mix into 2 large balls, squish into patties, and
.   place in the fridge to chill for 10 minutes.

Giant Black Bean Burger with Sweet Potato Fries

Ingredients

½ bell pepper

½ small yellow onion

2 garlic cloves

2 small sweet potatoes, or 1 large

2 tablespoons olive oil

1 teaspoon salt

Unsalted butter

2 burger buns

1 ripe avocado

Me

1. Preheat the oven to 425°F (215°C). Line a baking sheet with parchment paper. Set aside.

2. Finely dice the bell pepper, onion, and garlic. Hand them to YOU.

3. Slice the sweet potatoes lengthwise into thin, fry-shaped sticks. In a large bowl, toss with the olive oil and salt.

4. Lay the sweet potatoes on the prepared baking sheet and bake for 25 to 35 minutes, depending on how thick you've cut them. They should be cooked through and crispy. Keep the oven on and reduce the temperature to 400°F (200°C).

5. Rinse the leaves of the baby gem lettuce.

6. Butter the buns.

7. Scoop the flesh out of the avocado and mash it with a fork.

See next page for us directions.

Ingredients

2 tablespoons olive oil

2 slices sharp/mature cheddar cheese

1 head of baby gem lettuce

Us

1. In an ovenproof griddle pan or flat nonstick pan over medium heat, heat 1 tablespoon of the olive oil. Add the burgers straight from the fridge and cook for about 6 minutes on one side. Drizzle the remaining 1 tablespoon olive oil onto the top before flipping and cooking for another 3 minutes. Add the cheddar and finish in the hot oven for the final 3 to 4 minutes to melt it.

2. Remove the burgers from the pan and place the buns cut-side down on the hot pan to toast briefly.

3. Build your burgers with the lettuce and avocado and serve with the sweet potato fries on the side.

Chapter Two:

Veggie Soups, Noodles and Rice

My Favorite French Onion Soup

This classic French onion soup is quick to whip up together but needs about 30 minutes for the flavors to come together once the broth has been added to the caramelized onions. This is one of the longer recipes in this book; it takes about an hour total. This dish really benefits from a high-quality stock and since the other ingredients are so limited, I recommend skipping the stock cube/powder and splurging on some bone broth. This is a great time to get the dishes done early, open a bottle of wine (red, in my opinion), and play a quick game of cards. The scent of sweet onion and melted cheese will fill you up with anticipation that will make the payoff even better. I love this soup as a weeknight dinner, as it's very savoury but not so heavy that you can't sleep.

See recipe for one in the kitchen on page 179

For the Soup:

3 tablespoons unsalted butter

3 large yellow onions

2 garlic cloves

1 teaspoon sugar

4 cups (1 liter) good-quality beef,

vegetable, or chicken stock

¼ cup (60 ml) dry white wine

1 dried bay leaf

1 sprig of fresh thyme

1 tablespoon sherry vinegar

Salt and freshly ground black pepper,

to taste

For the Croutons:

1 tablespoon unsalted butter

½ baguette (French bread)

1½ cups (150 g) grated Gruyere cheese

Ingredients

You

3 large yellow onions

3 tablespoons unsalted butter

1 teaspoon sugar

Salt and freshly ground black pepper

1. Slice the onions as thinly as possible.

2. In a large, heavy-bottomed pot over medium heat, melt the butter and add the onions. Cook until softened, 10 minutes. Add the sugar and the garlic from ME. Increase the heat to medium-high and cook, browning the onions for another 20 minutes.

3. Add the stock, wine, bay leaf, and thyme from ME. Bring to a boil, scraping any browned onions at the bottom of the pot.

4. Reduce the heat, cover, and cook for 30 minutes.

5. Add the sherry vinegar and salt and pepper to taste.

Ingredients

2 garlic cloves

4 cups (1 liter) good-quality beef, vegetable, or chicken stock

¼ cup (60 ml) dry white wine

1 dried bay leaf

1 sprig of fresh thyme

1½ cups (150 g) grated Gruyere cheese

½ baguette (French bread)

1 tablespoon unsalted butter

Me

1.   Preheat the oven to the Broil/Grill setting at 450°F (230°C).

2.   Slice the garlic and hand to YOU.

3.   Measure the stock and combine with the white wine, thyme, and bay leaf in a bowl.

4.   Grate the cheese for the croutons.

5.   Slice the baguette into 4-inch pieces, then cut them in half lengthwise. Set aside.

6.   Butter one side of each baguette piece and place them on a baking sheet. Top each with one-quarter of the cheese, pressing to compact it onto the slices.

7.   Place these under the broiler for 3 to 5 minutes, until the cheese is bubbly and browned and the bread is toasted around the outside.

Us

1.   Spoon the soup into 2 bowls and serve each with 2 slices of cheesy bread.

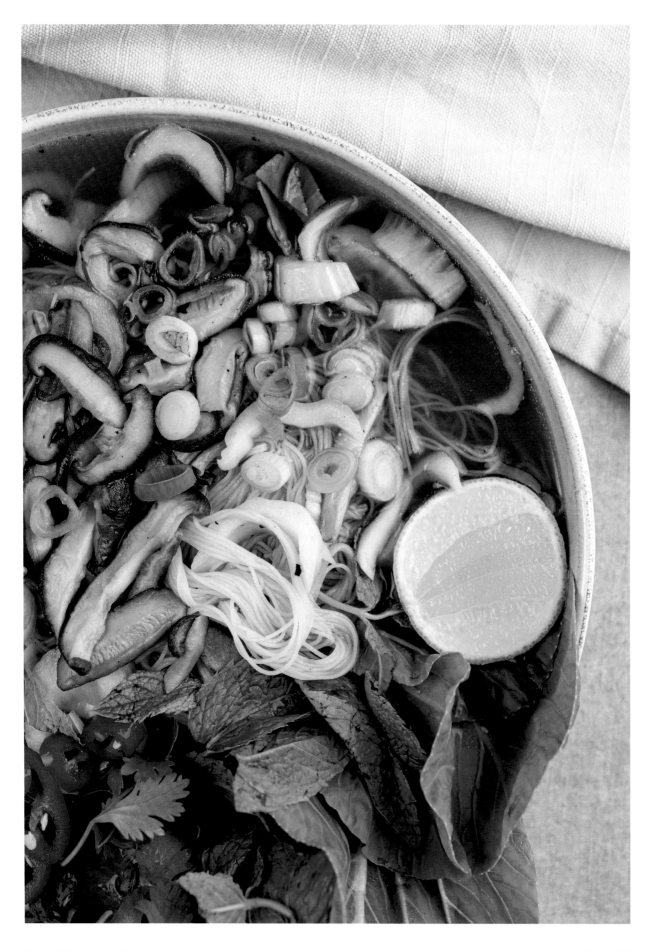

Vegan Mushroom Pho

Pho, or Vietnamese soup, is my comfort food. The combination of a rich broth made from caramelized vegetables and warming spices, noodles and fresh herbs suits just about any mood. It's always my first choice for a Sunday night delivery but it wasn't until I played around with making this rich vegetarian version that it became a home cooking staple. The ingredients are inexpensive and easy to find and with two of you on the job it whips together in about 30 minutes and tastes like you've been simmering it for hours. You can add other garnishes here if you like: grated carrots, bean sprouts etc. but I love the simplicity of the crisp bok-choi and the salty umami mushrooms.

See recipe for one in the kitchen on page 180

Ingredients

7 ounces (200 g) shiitake mushrooms or mixed mushrooms

3 scallions or spring onions

2 cups (480 ml) good-quality vegetable stock

3 star anise

3 whole cloves

1 cinnamon stick

1 tablespoon plus 1 teaspoon olive oil

1 large white onion

2 carrots

1-inch piece of fresh ginger

1 teaspoon salt, plus more as needed

4 ½ ounces (130 g) uncooked vermicelli rice noodles

1 tablespoon soy sauce or tamari, plus more to taste

2 heads of bok choy/ baby pak

1 handful (15 g) of fresh cilantro/coriander

1 handful (10 g) of fresh mint

1 to 2 birds-eye chilis (depending on your heat preference)

1 lime

Ingredients

2 cups (480 ml) good-quality vegetable stock

3 star anise

3 whole cloves

1 cinnamon stick

1 tablespoon plus 1 teaspoon olive oil

1 teaspoon salt, plus more as needed

You

1. In a large saucepan over high heat, add the vegetable stock and 2 cups (280 ml) of water. Add the star anise, cloves, and cinnamon stick and bring to a boil. Reduce to a low simmer.

2. In a skillet over high heat, heat 1 teaspoon olive oil along with the onion and carrots from ME. Cook until browned and caramelized, about 10 minutes.

3. Add the onion and carrots to your broth.

4. Add the mushroom stems, scallion quarters, and sliced ginger from ME to your broth. Allow to simmer for 20 minutes.

5. In the same skillet you cooked the onion in over high heat, heat the remaining 1 tablespoon olive oil. Add the salt and the sliced mushroom from ME, sautéing until starting to caramelize and tender, about 10 minutes. Remove and allow to cool. Set aside.

Ingredients

Me

1 large white onion

2 carrots

1-inch piece of fresh ginger

3 scallions or spring onions

7 ounces (200 g) shiitake mushrooms or mixed mushrooms, stems removed and reserved; thinly sliced

4 ½ ounces (130 g) uncooked vermicelli rice noodles

2 heads of bok choy/baby pak

1 handful (15 g) of fresh cilantro/coriander

1 handful (10 g) of fresh mint

1 lime

1 to 2 birds-eye chilis (depending on your heat preference)

1. Roughly chop the onion and carrots. Pass these to YOU.

2. Thinly slice the ginger and cut 2 of the scallions into quarters. Pass these to YOU.

3. Chop the stems off the mushrooms. Pass these to YOU. Thinly slice the mushrooms and pass these to YOU.

4. Pour boiling water over the rice noodles to cook until softened, about 8 minutes or according to package instructions. Drain into a colander.

5. Slice the bok choy into thin ribbons by cutting horizontally. Rinse well. Do the same with the remaining scallion. Set aside.

6. Pick the mint and cilantro/coriander leaves off the stems. Roughly chop the mint.

7. Cut the lime into wedges.

8. Thinly slice the chilis.

See next page for us directions.

Vegan Mushroom Pho

Ingredients

1 tablespoon soy sauce or tamari,
plus more to taste

Salt

Us

1. Drain the broth through a colander into a large bowl to remove the spices, onion, and mushroom stems. Pour it back into the saucepan. Add the soy sauce. Adjust the seasoning with more soy sauce and salt if needed.

2. Add the bok choy to the broth and bring to a boil before removing from the heat.

3. Place a handful of noodles in the bottom of 2 bowls.

4. Divide the cooked sliced mushrooms, sliced scallions, cilantro, mint, and chilis between the 2 bowls. Ladle the broth over the top. Squeeze lime over everything.

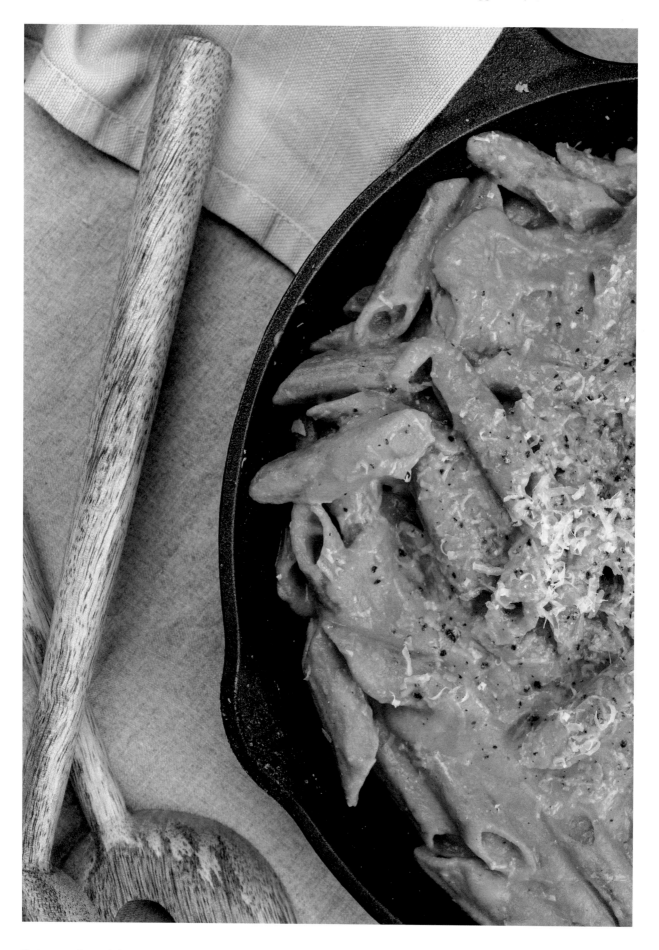

Butternut Squash Vodka Pasta

Butternut Squash Vodka Pasta

I love this recipe because it embodies the concept of "healthy comfort food" so perfectly. It's a classic and simple dish, but with the addition of the rich blended vegetables, you get a gorgeous, nutritious spin on it. It comes together in about 20 minutes, and it's a great recipe for your first time in the kitchen with a partner. I recommend serving this with a simple salad on the side. And maybe a vodka soda.

See recipe for one in the kitchen on page 181

Ingredients

4 tablespoons olive oil

½ butternut squash

6 tomatoes

2 garlic cloves

1 onion

2 tablespoons tomato paste

½ cup (100 ml) vodka

½ cup (100 ml) milk (I used almond milk)

2 cups (250 g) penne pasta

Salt and freshly ground black pepper

Grated Parmesan cheese, for serving

Ingredients

You

Parmesan cheese

4 tablespoons olive oil

2 tablespoons tomato paste

½ cup (100 ml) vodka

Salt and freshly ground black
pepper, to taste

½ cup (100 ml) milk (I use
almond milk)

1.   If your parmesan isn't grated, take this opportunity to grate
     enough to top 2 bowls of pasta to your taste.

2.   Pour 1 inch of water into the bottom of a large pan with a
     steamer basket (or with a metal strainer on top) and set on
     the stove over medium-high heat.

3.   Add the butternut squash prepared by ME and steam until
     soft, 15 minutes. Set aside.

4.   In a large pan over medium heat, heat the olive oil. Add the
     onion and garlic prepared by ME and cook slowly until cara-
     melized, about 10 minutes.

5.   Add the tomato paste and cook for another minute.

6.   Add the chopped tomatoes prepared by ME and the vodka
     and season with salt and pepper. Simmer until the tomatoes
     are soft.

7.   Add the soft butternut squash and the milk to the tomato
     mixture and cook together for 5 minutes.

Ingredients

½ butternut squash

1 onion

2 garlic cloves

6 tomatoes

2 cups (250 g) penne pasta

Me

1. Peel the butternut squash, remove the seeds and any stringy bits and slice in half. Chop into 1-inch chunks. Hand these to YOU.

2. Chop the onion and garlic into a small dice and hand to YOU.

3. Roughly chop the tomatoes and hand to YOU.

4. Bring a pot of salted water to a boil and cook the pasta according to package directions.

Us

1. In a blender or the bowl of a food processor, add the tomato-butternut squash mixture and blend until completely smooth. Pour over the pasta, mixing to combine.

2. Top with the grated Parmesan and pepper.

Sweet Potato Gnocchi with Red Pesto

Gnocchi is technically a pasta, but it has an incredible soft and pillowy texture that melts in your mouth. In my opinion, it's the perfect vegetarian dish: filling, hearty enough to satisfy any craving, and pairs beautifully with a variety of sauces and other vegetables. And, because it is potato-based, gnocchi is also easy to make gluten-free, making it a great option for those (like me!) with dietary restrictions.

Here you need to cook the sweet potato ahead. One person can do this in advance, or you can do it together and enjoy a cup of coffee or a glass of wine together while it bakes.

See recipe for one in the kitchen on page 182

For the Pesto:

½ cup (30 g) oil-packed sun-dried tomatoes

1/3 cup (70 g) extra-virgin olive oil (or use the sun-dried tomato oil instead for added flavor)

¼ cup (35 g) raw, unsalted cashews

¼ cup (25 g) grated Parmesan cheese

1 garlic clove

Juice of ½ lemon

⅛ teaspoon chili flakes (optional)

¼ teaspoon salt

Freshly ground black pepper

For the Gnocchi:

1 medium sweet potato

½ cup (125 g) ricotta cheese

¼ cup (25 g) grated Parmesan cheese

Salt

2/3 cup (85 g) all-purpose flour (gluten-free if needed), plus more for dusting

1 tablespoon olive oil

Ingredients

1 medium sweet potato

1/2 cup (50 g) grated Parmesan cheese

½ cup (30 g) oil-packed sun-dried toma-toes

1/3 cup (70 g) extra-virgin olive oil (or use the sun-dried tomato oil instead for added flavor)

¼ cup (35 g) raw, unsalted cashews

1 garlic clove

Juice of ½ lemon

⅛ teaspoon chili flakes (optional)

Salt and freshly ground black pepper

You

1. If you haven't pre-cooked your sweet potato, roast it by pre-heating the oven to 425F (215C). Line a baking sheet with foil. Use a fork to prick holes into the sweet potato. Place on the baking sheet and bake for about 45 minutes, until soft. Remove from the oven and let cool.

2. Grate the Parmesan cheese. Pass 2 tablespoons of the grated cheese to ME.

3. Scoop out the sweet potato flesh and pass to ME.

4. Make the pesto: In a blender or the bowl of a food processor, add the sun-dried tomatoes, olive oil, cashews, Parmesan, garlic, lemon juice, chili flakes (if using), ¼ teaspoon of salt, and the pepper to taste. Process until well incorporated. Set aside.

Ingredients

½ cup (125 g) ricotta cheese

Salt

2/3 cup (85 g) all-purpose flour (gluten-free if needed), plus more for dusting

Me

1. In a large bowl, combine the ricotta, 2 tablespoons of the Parmesan cheese from YOU, and a pinch of salt. Add the sweet potato flesh from YOU. Combine until smooth.

2. Measure 2/3 cup of the flour and sift it into a separate bowl.

3. Add the flour to the ricotta mixture and mix well with a spoon. Don't overmix; this ensures the dough remains slightly fluffy in texture.

Ingredients

Salt

1 tablespoon olive oil

Us

1. Lightly dust your work surface with flour.

2. Take a portion of the dough, similar in size to a
    tennis ball, and roll the dough with both hands
    into a long snake shape.

3. Cut into 1-inch pieces. Repeat until all the dough
    is used.

4. Bring a large pot of salted water to a boil. Add the
    gnocchi, working in batches so as not to over-
    crowd the pot. Allow to float to the surface before
    removing with a slotted spoon.

5. In a large skillet over high heat, heat the olive oil
    and pan-fry the finished gnocchi and add the pes-
    to to coat. Top with the remaining 2 tablespoons
    Parmesan cheese.

LA's Best Fried Tofu Bowl

A staple in my house, this healthy vegan comfort food presents a perfect opportunity to go plant-based for a weekday dinner. The leftovers make a great next-day lunch as well. The recipe combines nutrient-rich brown rice, crispy fried tofu, and kale with a mouth-watering tahini dressing. You end up with a super flavorful, crunchy, and satisfying bowl that will leave you feeling full yet energized. What I love about this recipe is it combines three of my favorite elements. I often whip up some of this crunchy kale and coconut on its own and add it to my daughter's lunchbox and the tahini dressing has a dedicated spot in my fridge because we use it on everything!

See recipe for one in the kitchen on page 183

Ingredients

1 cup (200 g) uncooked brown rice

1 medium bunch of curly kale

½ cup (50 g) unsweetened coconut flakes

1/3 cup (20 g) nutritional yeast

¼ teaspoon salt

2 tablespoons olive oil

For the Tofu:

One 16-ounce block firm or extra-firm tofu

2 tablespoons corn starch

½ teaspoon salt

½ teaspoon freshly ground black pepper

2 tablespoons vegetable oil

Lime wedges, for serving

For the Dressing:

1 lime

¼ cup (60 ml) olive oil

1 ½ tablespoons tahini

1 tablespoon soy sauce

1 tablespoon honey

1 teaspoon toasted sesame oil

Ingredients

1 cup (200 g) uncooked brown rice

½ cup (50 g) unsweetened coconut flakes

1/3 cup (20 g) nutritional yeast

¼ teaspoon salt

2 tablespoons olive oil

1 lime

¼ cup (60 ml) olive oil

1 ½ tablespoons tahini

1 tablespoon soy sauce

1 tablespoon honey

1 teaspoon toasted sesame oil

You

1. Preheat the oven to 375°F (190°C). Line a baking sheet with parchment paper and set aside.

2. In a small pot with a lid, add the rice and 2 cups (475 ml) of water. Bring the rice and water to a boil, then reduce the heat to a simmer, cover, and allow to cook until all the water is absorbed, about 20 minutes. Leaving the lid on, remove the pot from the heat and allow it to steam for another 10 minutes.

3. In a large bowl, toss the kale from ME, the coconut, nutritional yeast, salt, and olive oil. Place on the prepared baking sheet and roast, tossing halfway through, until the kale is crispy and the coconut is golden, about 10 minutes. Keep an eye on this to make sure your kale doesn't burn.

4. Make the dressing: Finely grate the zest from the lime directly into a small bowl. Halve the lime and squeeze in the juice.

5. Add the olive oil, tahini, soy sauce, honey, and sesame oil.

Ingredients

1 medium bunch of curly kale

One 16-ounce block firm or extra-firm tofu

2 tablespoons corn starch

½ teaspoon salt

½ teaspoon freshly ground black pepper

2 tablespoons vegetable oil

Me

1. Rinse the kale, remove the ribs and stems, and roughly chop the leaves. Pass these to YOU.

2. Remove the tofu from its packaging and place it on a plate. Use paper towels or a clean kitchen towel to gently press out the excess liquid from the tofu block. You can also use a tofu press if you have one.

3. Cut the tofu into 1-inch cubes.

4. In a large bowl, combine the corn starch with a teaspoon salt and pepper and mix well. Add the tofu cubes to the bowl and toss to coat evenly.

5. Line a plate with paper towels. Set aside.

6. In a nonstick skillet or cast-iron pan over medium-high heat, heat the vegetable oil. Add the coated tofu cubes, spread them out in the pan, and let them cook without moving them for 3 to 4 minutes. Flip the tofu cubes and cook until golden brown and crispy on all sides, another 3 to 4 minutes.

7. Remove the tofu from the pan and drain onto the prepared plate.

Us

Lime wedges

1   In a large bowl, toss the rice with the crispy kale, coconut, and tofu. Add the dressing and toss until everything is combined.

2.. Split between 2 bowls and serve with lime wedges.

Kimchee Fried Forbidden Rice Bowl

This recipe was inspired by a dish I loved at one of my favorite yoga studios in LA. It's a hearty and warming meal, but also packed with healthy ingredients and bursting with flavor. It works great as a quick 30-minute dinner when split between two people. You can cut the time down even more by using leftover rice. Kimchee, a traditional Korean side dish made from fermented cabbage, radish, and various spices, is not only incredibly delicious, but also great for gut health, making it a fantastic addition to your fridge. The combination of tangy and spicy flavors from the kimchee, paired with the nutty flavor of fried rice, creates a perfectly balanced dish. If you can't find black or forbidden rice, sometimes also called Venus rice, you can use any rice here and just follow the cooking instructions off the package.

See recipe for one in the kitchen on page 184

For the Rice:

1 cup (200 g) uncooked black/forbidden or jasmine rice

2 tablespoons olive oil

1 small onion

2 garlic cloves

2 cups (150 g) shiitake mushrooms

2 bunches of baby bok choy/pak choi

1 cup (150 g) kimchee

Salt and freshly ground black pepper, to taste

For Serving:

1 sheet nori (seaweed)

2 scallions or spring onions

1 tablespoon sesame seeds

For the Sauce:

2 tablespoons soy sauce

1 tablespoon gochujang sauce, plus more for serving (you can also use chili garlic sauce here)

1 tablespoon toasted sesame oil

½-inch piece of fresh ginger

For the Eggs:

1 tablespoon toasted sesame oil

1 teaspoon gochujang sauce (you can use chili garlic sauce here if you can't find gochujang)

2 large eggs

Salt

Ingredients

You

2 tablespoons soy sauce

1 tablespoon gochujang sauce, plus
more for serving (you can also use
chili garlic sauce here)

1 tablespoon toasted sesame oil

½-inch piece of fresh ginger

1 cup (200 g) uncooked black/forbid-
den or jasmine rice

2 tablespoons olive oil

Salt and freshly ground black pepper,
to taste

1.   Make the sauce: In a small bowl, whisk together the soy
     sauce, gochujang, and sesame oil. Grate in the ginger and
     combine. Set aside.

2.   Make the rice: In a medium pot with a lid, combine the rice
     with 2 cups (470 ml) water. Bring to a boil, place the lid on
     the pot, and cook until the water has all been absorbed.
     The cook time will depend on the type of rice used, so
     check the package for instructions. Remove from the heat.
     Leave covered for another 10 minutes.

3.   In a large skillet over medium heat, heat the olive oil. Add
     the onion and garlic from ME. Cook until the onion is trans-
     lucent, about 5 minutes.

4.   Add the mushrooms from ME and increase the heat so
     they are crisping up slightly in the pan. Make sure the
     onions and garlic are not burning.

5.   Once these are crisped but tender on the inside, 5 to 7
     minutes more, add the sliced bok choy and kimchee from
     ME and cook until the bok choy has wilted slightly, another
     2 minutes.

6.   Scrape any browned bits off the bottom of the pan using
     the liquid from the kimchee and bok choy.

7.   Add the cooked rice and the sauce and increase the heat
     slightly to fry it all together for 5 minutes. Add salt and
     pepper to taste. Remove from the heat.

Ingredients

Me

1 small onion

2 garlic cloves

2 cups (150 g) shiitake mushrooms

2 bunches of baby bok choy/pak choi

1 cup (150 g) kimchee

1 sheet nori (seaweed)

2 scallions or spring onions

1 tablespoon toasted sesame oil

1 teaspoon gochujang sauce (you can use chili garlic sauce here if you can't find gochujang)

2 large eggs

Salt

1. Finely chop the garlic and onion. Pass to YOU.

2. Remove the stems from the mushrooms. Quarter the mushrooms and pass to YOU.

3. Rinse the bok choy, trim the ends, and slice horizontally into thin strips. Pass to YOU.

4. Drain and roughly chop the kimchee and pass it to YOU.

5. Thinly slice the scallions.

6. Use scissors to cut the nori sheet into thin strips.

7. In a nonstick or cast-iron skillet over medium-high heat, heat the sesame oil and gochujang until both are sizzling. Gently mix with the back of a spoon so the gochujang is evenly distributed.

8. Crack the eggs into the sauce and cook until the whites are set but the yolks are still runny, 2 to 3 minutes. Season with salt.

Us

1 tablespoon sesame seeds

1. Spoon the fried rice into 2 bowls. Top with the fried eggs. Sprinkle the scallions, nori strips, and sesame seeds over the top.

James' Butternut Squash Curry

This decadent sweet potato and butternut squash curry is a weeknight regular in our house. It's my husband's favorite dish to make and he makes huge batches of it so we always have extra in the fridge. He likes to serve the sweet potato and squash chunky, but I like them mashed slightly, so I've added that to the recipe, but if you prefer the chunks and a thinner broth, you can skip that last step. I usually serve this with extra chili sauce and a dollop of yogurt.

See recipe for one in the kitchen on page 187

Ingredients

1 cup brown rice

1 large shallot

2 garlic cloves

1 to 2 red chilis (depending on heat preference)

1-inch piece of fresh ginger

Salt

1 tablespoon olive oil

2 teaspoons ground turmeric

1 teaspoon ground cumin

1 teaspoon ground coriander

One 14-ounce (400 ml) can full-fat coconut milk

One 14-ounce (400 ml) can chopped tomatoes

2 large, sweet potatoes

1 small or ½ large butternut squash

2 large handfuls of baby spinach

¼ bunch of fresh cilantro/coriander

Lime wedges, for serving

½ cup Greek yogurt, for serving

Ingredients

You

1 large shallot, peeled

2 garlic cloves, peeled

1 to 2 red chilis (depending on heat preference)

1-inch piece of fresh ginger

Salt

1 tablespoon olive oil

2 teaspoons ground turmeric

1 teaspoon ground cumin

1 teaspoon ground coriander

1 teaspoon salt

2 large handfuls of baby spinach

1.   In a blender or the bowl of a food processor, add the shallot, garlic, chilis, ginger, a large pinch of salt, and ½ cup (100 ml) water. Blend to a fine paste.

2.   In a large pot over medium heat, heat the olive oil. Add the shallot paste and cook until the liquid has mostly evaporated and the paste is sputtering, 5 to 8 minutes.

3.   Add the turmeric, cumin, and ground coriander. Cook until fragrant, 30 seconds.

4.   Add the coconut milk and tomato from ME. Add 1 teaspoon salt. Bring to a boil and reduce to a simmer.

5.   Add the chopped squash and sweet potato from ME to the pot. If there is not enough liquid to cover the vegetables, add just enough water until they are submerged. Cover and cook for 30 minutes.

6.   Rinse the spinach.

Ingredients

1 cup brown rice

One 14-ounce (400 ml) can full-fat coconut milk

One 14-ounce (400 ml) can chopped tomatoes

2 large sweet potatoes

1 small or ½ large butternut squash

¼ bunch of fresh cilantro/coriander

Me

1. In a medium pot with a lid, combine the rice with 2 cups (470 ml) water. Bring to a boil, cover with a lid, and allow to simmer for 20 minutes, or until cooked through. Remove from the heat. Leave the lid on to steam the rice.

2. Open the cans of coconut milk and tomatoes. Hand these to YOU.

3. Peel the sweet potatoes. Roughly chop into 1-inch chunks. Cut the squash in half and spoon the seeds and any stringy bits out. Roughly chop into 1-inch chunks. Hand these to YOU.

4. Roughly chop the cilantro and cut the lime into wedges.

Us

½ cup Greek yogurt

Lime wedges

Salt

1. If you want to mash the squash and potato, use a fork or potato masher to gently mash the curry.

2. Fold in the baby spinach.

3. Serve hot over the rice. Serve with the chopped cilantro and lime wedges. Top with a dollop of yogurt.

Chapter Three:

Seafood

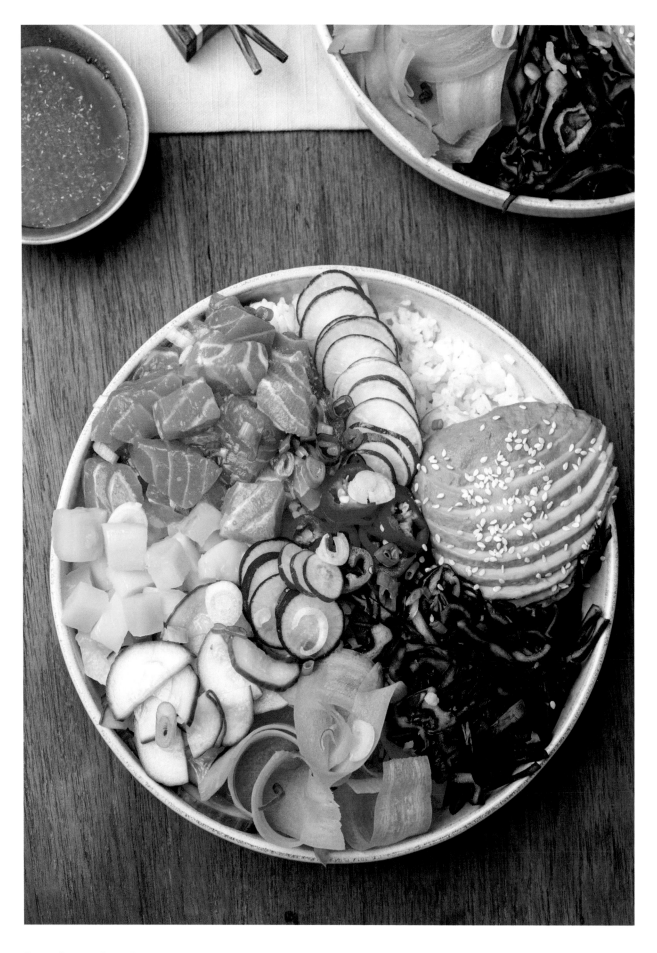

Fresh Salmon Poke Bowls

One of my first ever Cook Together recipes (over five years before the publication of this book), this poke bowl is a treat. Poke is originally from Hawaii, where cooks use the off-cuts of high-quality sushi to put together a more affordable fresh fish meal. If you can't find sushi-grade salmon, you can use any salmon and just poach it slightly in the sauce (cook slowly in a small saucepan over low heat). Part of the fun of this dish is practicing your knife skills, beautifully cutting, prepping, and layering the ingredients in the bowl for a photo-worthy presentation.

See recipe for one in the kitchen on page 188

Ingredients

1 cup (200 g) uncooked white rice

2 tablespoons rice vinegar

1 tablespoon sugar

½ cucumber

¼ small purple cabbage

Salt

5 tablespoons tamari or soy sauce

1 ½ tablespoons toasted sesame oil

Pinkie finger-size piece of fresh ginger

For the Sauce:

4 scallions or spring onions

2/3 pound (300 g) sushi-grade salmon (or tuna)

6 radishes

1 carrot

1 avocado

1 chili (optional)

1 mango

Ingredients

1 cup (200 g) uncooked white rice

2 tablespoons rice vinegar

1 tablespoon sugar

5 tablespoons tamari or soy sauce

1 ½ tablespoons toasted sesame oil

Pinkie finger-size piece of fresh ginger

You

1. Run the rice under cold water until it starts to run clear. In a medium pot with a lid, combine the rice with 2 cups (470 ml) water. Bring to a boil, reduce to a simmer, and cover with a lid for 10 minutes, or until the rice is cooked and the water is absorbed. Remove from the heat. Leave the lid on to steam the rice.

2. In a small pan, combine the rice wine vinegar, ½ cup (110 ml) water, and the sugar. Bring to a boil and remove from the heat.

3. Add the sliced cucumber to the pan and set aside for at least 15 minutes to pickle.

4. In a large bowl, whisk together the soy sauce and sesame oil. Grate the ginger into the sauce and add the scallions from ME.

5. Toss the cut salmon from ME in the soy-sesame sauce and place in the fridge until you are ready to serve.

Ingredients

½ cucumber

4 scallions or spring onions

2/3 pound (300 g) sushi-grade salmon (or tuna)

¼ small purple cabbage

Salt

6 radishes

1 carrot

1 avocado

1 chili (optional)

1 mango (optional)

Me

1. Thinly slice the cucumber and pass to YOU.

2. Thinly slice the white and light green parts of the scallions. Pass to YOU.

3. Remove the skin from the salmon (if there is any) and cut it into small cubes. Pass to YOU.

4   Thinly slice the purple cabbage and massage it slightly with a pinch of salt. Place it in a colander over the sink to allow the excess liquid to run off.

5. Slice the radishes. Thinly slice the carrot. Set aside.

6. Remove the pit of the avocado, scoop out the flesh, and slice lengthwise. Set aside.

7. Peel the mango and cut into small cubes (if using).

8. Thinly slice the chili (if using).

Us

1. Pour the excess liquid off the cabbage and the pickled cucumbers.

2. If cooking the salmon, pour the contents of the sauce and salmon into a small pot and cook slowly over low heat, stirring gently once, until the salmon turns opaque, 5 to 10 minutes. Otherwise, serve raw.

3. Assemble the bowls: Top the rice with the salmon (pour extra sauce over the rice), the pickled cucumber, cabbage, radishes, carrot, and avocado. Top with the mango and chili (if using).

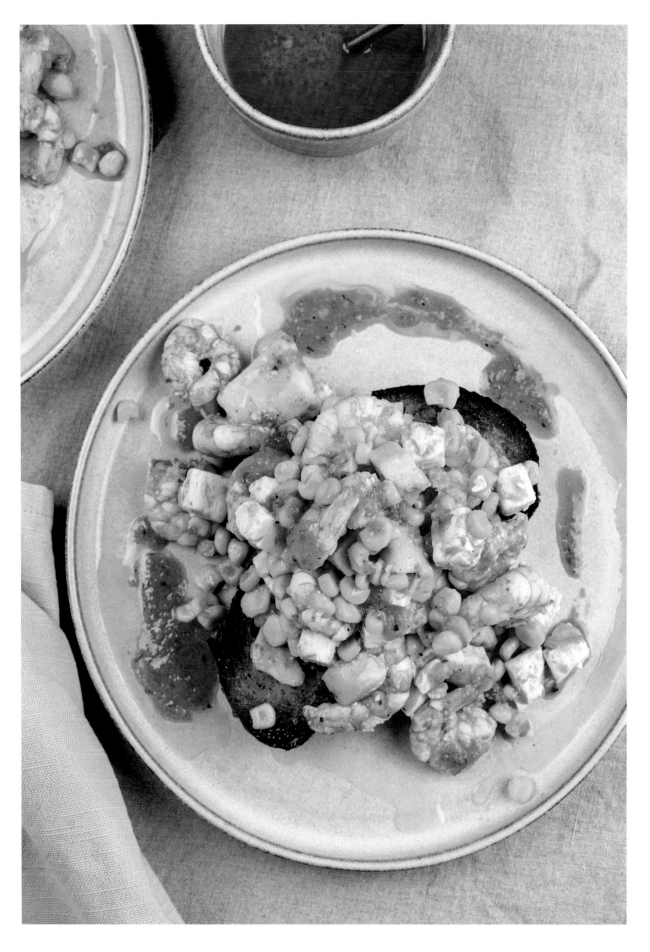

Grilled Peri-Peri Prawns with Sweet Corn, Avocado, and Feta

Grilled Peri-Peri Prawns with Sweet Corn, Avocado, and Feta

Warning: This spicy recipe might have you booking a one-way ticket to South Africa.
In this dish, juicy, pan-fried prawns are marinated in a homemade peri-peri sauce made with a blend of fiery African bird's eye chilis, garlic, bell pepper, and spices. The corn adds a touch of sweetness to the dish, the avocado and feta a rich and buttery contrast. It's easy to make, but the result looks and tastes like a gourmet, restaurant-quality meal.

See recipe for one in the kitchen on page 189

For the Peri Peri Sauce:

1 red bell pepper

3 red bird's eye chilis

8 unpeeled garlic cloves

½ cup (120 ml) extra-virgin olive oil

3 tablespoons red or white wine vinegar

2 teaspoons salt

½ teaspoon smoked paprika

For the Prawns:

1 pound (450 g) raw jumbo prawns (these can be fresh or frozen)

1 tablespoon olive oil

2 cups (328 g) frozen corn

1 ripe avocado

7 ounces (200 g) feta cheese

1 tablespoon unsalted butter

2 large slices sourdough toast

1 lime

Ingredients

1 red bell pepper

3 red bird's eye chilis

8 unpeeled garlic cloves

1 tablespoon unsalted butter

2 large slices sourdough toast

You

1. Preheat the oven to the Broil/Grill setting at 450°F (230°C). Place an oven rack in the top third of the oven.

2. Quarter the bell pepper, removing the stem and seeds. Trim the stems off the chilis.

3. Place the bell pepper, chilis, and garlic on an oven tray and place under the broiler/grill. Cook until starting to char, 5 minutes. Remove and flip to cook the other side under the broiler. Continue to grill/broil until charred all over, another 5 minutes. Remove and allow to cool.

4. Peel the garlic once it's cooled slightly.

5. Add the peppers and the garlic to the blender prepared by ME to make the peri-peri sauce. Blend. Transfer half of the sauce to a large bowl and reserve the rest. Set aside.

6. Add the cleaned prawns to the bowl with half of the sauce, tossing to coat. Set aside.

7. Butter the sourdough and set aside.

Ingredients

Me

½ cup (120 ml) extra-virgin olive oil

3 tablespoons red or white wine vinegar

2 teaspoons salt

½ teaspoon smoked paprika

1 pound (450 g) raw jumbo prawns (these can be fresh or frozen)

1 ripe avocado

7 ounces (200 g) feta cheese

1 lime

2 cups (328 g) frozen corn

1. In a blender, add the olive oil, vinegar, paprika, and salt. Set aside for YOU.

2. If your prawns are frozen, run them under room-temperature water for a few minutes until defrosted.

3. Peel and devein the prawns if needed: Starting from the head end, use your thumb or a small knife to loosen the shell from the body. Peel the shell off by pulling it down and away from the body. Once the shell is removed, you'll see a black or brown vein running down the back of the prawn. You can remove it by making a shallow incision down the back of the prawn with a sharp knife and pulling the vein out with your fingers.

4. Rinse the prawns and pat dry. Pass these to YOU.

5. Remove the pit from the avocado, use a spoon to scoop the flesh out, and cut into small cubes. Add to a large bowl.

6. Cut the feta into cubes the same size as the avocado and add to the bowl with the avocado.

7. Halve the lime.

8. Thaw the frozen corn by placing in a colander and rinsing it under warm water. Set aside.

See next page for us directions.

Grilled Peri-Peri Prawns with Sweet Corn, Avocado, and Feta

Ingredients

1 tablespoon olive oil

Salt

Us

1. In a large skillet over high heat, heat the olive oil and add the thawed corn with a pinch of salt. Continue to cook, stirring until the corn is starting to char and pop (this should happen quickly). Remove from the pan, allow to cool, and add to the bowl with the feta and avocado.

2. In the same skillet you used for the corn over high heat, add the coated prawns. Cook until curling up and opaque, 1 to 2 minutes per side.

3. Stir the prawns into the corn, avocado, and feta mixture.

4. Add the bread to the same pan over medium-high heat, butter-side down, until you have a nice, toasted side.

5. Remove and place on 2 plates, toasted-side up.

6. Top with the prawn salad. Drizzle more sauce over it if you like things very spicy. Squeeze the lime juice over the top.

Baja-Style Fish Tacos with Fresh Corn Tortillas

Baja-Style Fish Tacos with Fresh Corn Tortillas

This is the perfect meal. It's a fact. These Baja-style fish tacos have such a clean, balanced flavor that you'll be transported to the beach with every bite. I use a light almond coating for the fish, which adds protein and a toasted nuttiness, but you can substitute breadcrumbs here; they are easier to find and less expensive. The freshness of the slaw with the pan-fried fish and the simple roasted salsa come together perfectly, in true Mexican style. You have an option at the end to make your own corn tortillas, a perfect job for two people to do together – although you'll want a tortilla press – but store-bought ones are great too.

See recipe for one in the kitchen on page 190

For the Fish:

½ cup (50 g) almond flour

1 teaspoon paprika

½ teaspoon garlic powder

Salt

1/3 cup (45 g) gluten-free or all-purpose flour

1 large egg

Olive oil

12 ounces (340 g) cod

Fresh Tortillas, for serving (recipe follows), or 8 store-bought tortillas

For the Slaw:

1 handful of cilantro/coriander

¼ cup (70 g) plain Greek yogurt

Zest and juice of 1/2 lime

Salt

1/2 small red cabbage

For the Salsa:

3 to 4 medium tomatoes

1/2 onion

1 red chili

1 unpeeled garlic clove

Juice of 1 lime

1 teaspoon cumin seeds

½ teaspoon honey

½ teaspoon salt

For the Fresh Tortillas (optional):

Makes 8 to 10 tortillas

1 ½ cups (90 g) masa harina

1 cup (120 ml) water

Ingredients

¼ cup (70 g) plain Greek yogurt

Zest and juice of 1/2 lime

Salt, to taste

½ cup (50 g) almond flour

1 teaspoon paprika

½ teaspoon garlic powder

Salt

1/3 cup (45 g) gluten-free or all-purpose flour

1 large egg

12 ounces (340 g) cod

Olive oil

You

1. Prepare 3 bowls to bread the fish: In a large, shallow bowl, whisk together the almond flour, paprika, garlic powder, and a large pinch of salt. In a separate shallow bowl, add the gluten-free flour. In a third shallow bowl, add and whisk the egg.

2. Cut the cod into 1 ½-inch strips and pat dry.

3. Dip the fish first in the gluten-free flour, shaking to remove excess, then in the egg and then in the almond flour mixture.

4. Preheat a frying pan over medium-high heat, covering the base of the pan about ½ inch (1 cm) of olive oil.

5. Working in batches, pan-fry the fish until golden, about 2 minutes per side. Repeat with all the strips.

6. In a medium bowl, combine the yoghurt with the lime zest and juice. Season with salt to taste. Add the cabbage and cilantro from ME and toss to make the slaw.

Ingredients

1 handful of cilantro/coriander

1/2 small red cabbage

1/2 onion

3 to 4 medium tomatoes

1 red chili

1 unpeeled garlic clove

Juice of 1 lime

1 teaspoon cumin seeds

½ teaspoon honey

½ teaspoon salt

Me

1.   Turn on the broiler/grill to its hottest setting.

2.   Separate the cilantro leaves from their stems. Save the stems for the salsa. Thinly slice the cabbage and combine with the cilantro leaves. Pass to YOU.

3.   Cut the onion half in half.

4.   Place the tomatoes, onion quarters, chili, and garlic on the prepared baking sheet and cook under the broiler/grill until blistered, tossing halfway through, 5 to 10 minutes. Allow to cool.

5.   Peel the tomatoes and garlic. Discard the skins.

6.   In a blender or food processor, add the tomatoes, onions, chili garlic, lime juice, cumin seeds, honey, salt, and the reserved cilantro stems. Blend to your desired consistency. Set aside.

Us

Tortillas, for serving (recipe follows), or 8 store-bought tortillas

1.   If making tortillas, make tortillas (see next page) or just heat store-bought tortillas in the warm oven.

2.   Build the tacos by placing the fish on the tortillas and topping with the slaw and salsa.

Fresh Tortillas

Ingredients

1 ½ cups (90 g) masa harina

1 cup (120 ml) water

You

1. In a large bowl, stir together the masa harina and water.

2. Knead together until you have a smooth, even texture.

3. Form small balls and press them between both sides of the tortilla press to form a flat tortilla. Pass these to ME to cook.

4. Repeat with the rest of the dough.

Me

1. Set up the tortilla press by putting cling wrap over both sides.

2. Set up 2 skillets, preferably nonstick or cast-iron, on the stove. One should be over medium heat and the other over high heat.

3. In the high-heat pan, cook the pressed tortilla the YOU has passed to you for 30 seconds. Use a spatula to flip it onto the second, medium-heat pan and cook the other side for another 30 seconds. Flip again onto the first side in the same medium-heat pan. Remove from the heat after a final 30 seconds.

Tuna Tataki Niçoise Salad

The French do a warm salad particularly well, and this jammy-egged Niçoise with seared tuna tataki on top is a great modification on the classic. I particularly adore tuna tataki, specifically with this toasted nigella seed crust. It adds a global touch to a classically southern French dish. This salad is not just for summer, though. It also makes a lovely, quick winter lunch or dinner. If you feel you are lacking carbohydrates, toss in some boiled new potatoes for a more filling version.

See recipe for one in the kitchen on page 192

For the Salad:

3 large eggs

6 ounces (300 g) tuna steak

1 small head of broccoli

7 ounces (200 g) green beans

1 head baby gem lettuce

7 ounces (200 g) cherry tomatoes

1 tablespoon olive oil

Sesame and nigella seeds, for serving

For the Dressing:

¼ cup (50 g) pitted olives (I like Castelvetrano, but black Niçoise are the classic)

2 ½ tablespoons olive oil

1 tablespoon red wine vinegar

Juice of ½ lemon

1 garlic clove

Salt and freshly ground black pepper

For the Tuna Rub:

1 tablespoon nigella (black onion) seeds

1 tablespoon white sesame seeds

½ teaspoon salt

Ingredients

Salt and freshly ground black pepper

3 large eggs

6 ounces (300 g) tuna steak

3 1/2 tablespoons olive oil

¼ cup (50 g) pitted olives (I like Castelvetrano, but black Niçoise are the classic)

1 tablespoon red wine vinegar

Juice of ½ lemon

1 garlic clove

You

1. Bring a medium pot of water to a boil.

2. Fill 2 bowls with ice and cold water. Set aside.

3. Use a spoon to slowly lower the eggs into the boiling water without breaking. Remove the eggs after 6 1/2 minutes and allow to cool in one of the ice baths.

4. Cut the tuna into rectangular blocks that are about 2 to 3 inches in length. The more rectangular the pieces, the easier it will be to cook. Pat the fish dry.

5. Rub the seed and salt mixture from ME gently over the tuna, creating a crust.

6. In a skillet over medium heat, heat the olive oil. Add the tuna slices and cook one side for 30 seconds. Flip onto the side to cook for another 30 seconds. Continue this until all 4 edges are equally cooked. The middle should still be raw. Place the fish on a plate and into the fridge to stop the cooking.

7. In a blender or bowl of a food processor, add the olives, olive oil, vinegar, lemon juice, and garlic. Add salt and pepper to taste.

.

Ingredients

Me

1 tablespoon nigella (black onion) seeds

1 tablespoon white sesame seeds

½ teaspoon salt

1 small head of broccoli

7 ounces (200 g) green beans

1 head baby gem lettuce

7 ounces (200 g) cherry tomatoes

1. In a small bowl, combine the nigella seeds, sesame seeds, and salt. Pass to YOU.

2. Cut the florets off the head of the broccoli and then further into small 1- to 1 ½-inch (3- to 4-cm) pieces.

3. Trim the ends off the green beans and cut them in half horizontally.

4. Cut the baby gem lettuce into small, even pieces.

5. Halve the cherry tomatoes.

6. Bring a large pot of salted water to a boil. Add the broccoli and cook until a butter knife slides through, 3 to 5 minutes. Transfer to the second ice bath that YOU has prepared. Keep the boiling water.

7. Add the green beans to the boiling water for 1 minute. Transfer to the ice bath with the broccoli and drain both into a colander.

See next page for us directions.

Ingredients

Sesame and nigella seeds

Us

1. Remove the cooled eggs from the ice water. Carefully peel them and cut in half.

2. Remove the tuna from the fridge and slice thinly to reveal the pink center.

3. Toss the lettuce, the broccoli, green beans, and cherry tomatoes with the dressing.

4. Divide between 2 plates and top with the sliced tuna, eggs, and sesame and nigella seeds.

Vietnamese-Style Shrimp & Rice Noodle Salad

Vietnamese food is the queen of cuisines. It's got many of the flavors and ingredients of other Southeast Asian cooking but a unique freshness from its abundance of herbs and raw or lightly cooked vegetables. It relies less on frying and more on refreshingly delicate options like rice paper and rice noodles. This salad is the perfect nod to the singularity of Vietnamese cooking, without too much technical skill required. You'll know the shrimp are cooked through when they go from clear to opaque (white) and become firm to the touch. Tip: Shrimp are better in this recipe, and most others, if cooked quickly, on high heat, to crisp the outside slightly.

See recipe for one in the kitchen on page 193

For the Shrimp:

½ pound (250 g) fresh or frozen raw shrimp/prawns (I like jumbo), peeled and deveined

½ bunch of fresh mint

½ bunch of fresh cilantro/coriander

1 large shallot

3 garlic cloves

1 red chili (optional)

Juice of 1 lime

2 tablespoons brown sugar

1 tablespoon olive oil

1 tablespoon fish sauce

½ tablespoon soy sauce (gluten-free if needed)

For the Salad:

7 ounces (200 g) uncooked rice vermicelli noodles

1 large carrot

1 red bell pepper

1 small cucumber

1 head baby gem lettuce

For the Nuoc Cham Dressing:

2 garlic cloves

1 chili

¼ cup (120 ml) fish sauce

Juice of 1 lime

2 tablespoons rice vinegar

1 tablespoon brown sugar

½ cup (120 ml) cold water

1 red chili, for serving

Fresh mint sprigs, for serving

Ingredients

½ pound (250 g) fresh or frozen raw
shrimp/prawns (I like jumbo), peeled
and deveined
1 large carrot
1 red bell pepper
1 small cucumber
1 head of baby gem lettuce
1 tablespoon olive oil

You

1.   Rinse the prawns under cold water.

2.   Peel and devein the prawns if needed: Starting from the
      head end, use your thumb or a small knife to loosen the
      shell from the body. Peel the shell off by pulling it down and
      away from the body. Once the shell is removed, you'll see
      a black or brown vein running down the back of the prawn.
      You can remove it by making a shallow incision down the
      back of the prawn with a sharp knife and pulling the vein
      out with your fingers.

3.   Rinse again. In a large bowl, add the prawns and toss with
      the marinade from ME. Place in the refrigerator to marinate
      for at least 10 minutes while you make the salad.

4.   Peel the carrot and cut it into long, thin matchsticks. You
      can also grate them.

5.   Remove the seeds from the bell pepper and cucumber and
      cut into long, thin matchsticks.

6.   Peel the leaves off the baby gem. Stack them on top of
      each other and slice them into thin ribbons.

7.   Add the carrot, bell pepper, cucumber, lettuce, mint leaves,
      and cilantro leaves to the bowl with the cooked rice noo-
      dles from ME.

8.   In a frying pan over high heat, heat the olive oil. Add the
      shrimp. Flip after 1 minute. They should cook through
      quickly, get a crispy exterior, and turn from clear to opaque
      (white). Toss the shrimp once more to ensure they cook
      evenly and remove from the heat. They should take about
      3 minutes total.

04

Ingredients

½ bunch of fresh mint

½ bunch of fresh cilantro/coriander

1 large shallot, peeled

5 garlic cloves, peeled

2 red chilis (optional)

Juice of 2 limes

3 tablespoons brown sugar

¼ cup plus 1 tablespoon fish sauce

½ tablespoon soy sauce (gluten-free if needed)

7 ounces (200 g) uncooked rice vermicelli noodles

Me

1. Boil water in a kettle.

2. Separate the leaves from the stems of the mint and cilantro. Reserve the mint and cilantro leaves for the salad and pass to YOU. Reserve the mint and cilantro stems.

3. In a blender or the bowl of a food processor, add the mint and cilantro stems along with the shallot, 3 of the garlic cloves, 1 chili (if using), half of the lime juice, 2 tablespoons of brown sugar, the olive oil, 1 tablespoon of fish sauce, and the soy sauce. This is your marinade. Pass to YOU.

4. In a large bowl, add the vermicelli noodles and soak in the boiling water for 5 minutes, or until they are tender. Drain into a colander and rinse with cold water until the noodles are room temperature. Return to the bowl. Pass to YOU.

5. Make the salad dressing: Finely chop the remaining 3 garlic cloves and the remaining 1 chili. In a small bowl, whisk together the garlic, chili, the remaining lime juice, the remaining ¼ cup fish sauce, the remaining 1 tablespoon brown sugar, the rice vinegar, and ½ cup cold water.

See next page for us directions.

Ingredients

Us

1 red chili, sliced, for serving

Fresh mint sprigs, for serving

1. Assemble the salad by tossing the noodles and vegetables with the dressing.

2. Top with the cooked prawns, sliced chili, and mint sprigs, and enjoy at room temperature.

Vietnamese-Style Shrimp & Rice Noodle Salad   Page 108

Pomegranate Salmon with Jewelled Rice

This is a take on a celebratory Iranian dish served at weddings and special occasions. The fruit and nuts create a 'jewelled' look for this rice and the fresh pomegranate seeds and glazed salmon are the icing on top. There are a few ingredients in here that are on the more expensive side, pomegranate molasses, pine nuts, apricots etc. so this really is a dish to save for a special occasion. You can swap out the dried fruits for others and the pine nuts for pistachios or sliced almonds if you prefer! The recipe works beautifully for two with ME prepping the ingredients so that YOU can get everything quickly in the pan and cooking.

See recipe for one in the kitchen on page 194

For the Rice:

2 tablespoons (30 g) unsalted butter

1 carrot

1 onion

½ cup (70 g) pine nuts

1 cinnamon stick

3 whole cloves

3 cardamom pods

1 star anise

1 cup (180 g) uncooked basmati rice

1/3 cup (50 g) raisins

¼ cup (50 g) apricots

½ cup (87 g) fresh pomegranate seeds, for serving

For the Salmon:

2 tablespoons pomegranate molasses

1 tablespoon olive oil

Juice of ½ lime

½ teaspoon salt

Two 4-ounce salmon filets (225 g)

Ingredients

2 tablespoons pomegranate molasses

1 tablespoon olive oil

Juice of ½ lime

½ teaspoon salt

Two 4-ounce salmon filets (225 g)

2 tablespoons (30 g) unsalted butter

1 cup (180 g) uncooked basmati rice

You

1. In a large bowl, whisk together the pomegranate molasses, olive oil, lime juice, and salt.

2. Toss the salmon filets in this mixture, cover, and refrigerate while you make the rice.

3. In a large skillet or pot with a lid over medium-high heat, melt the butter. Add the onion and carrot from ME and cook until browning, about 10 minutes. Remove from the pan.

4. In the same skillet over medium-high heat, add the pine nuts, cinnamon stick, cloves, cardamom, and star anise from ME and toast for 2 minutes.

5. Add the rice and cook for another minute with the spices. Return the cooked onion and carrot to the skillet. Stir to combine.

6. Add the raisins and chopped apricots from ME.

7. Pour 1 ¼ cups (300 ml) water over the top and fit with a lid. Cook on very low heat for 12 minutes. Remove from the heat and let sit, covered, for another 10 minutes.

Ingredients

Me

1 carrot

1 onion

½ cup (70 g) pine nuts

1 cinnamon stick

3 whole cloves

3 cardamom pods

1 star anise

1/3 cup (50 g) raisins

¼ cup (50 g) apricots

1. Preheat the oven to 400°F (200°C). Line a baking sheet with parchment paper. Set aside.

2. Grate the carrot and thinly slice the onion. Hand these to YOU.

3. Measure out the cinnamon stick, cloves, cardamom, star anise and pine nuts into a bowl and pass to YOU.

4. Chop the apricots. Add these to a bowl with the raisins and hand to YOU.

5. Take the salmon prepared by YOU out of the fridge and allow it to come to room temperature.

6. Place it on the prepared baking sheet, reserving the marinade left in the bowl, and bake for 10 minutes, or until cooked through.

7. Pour the remaining marinade from the salmon into a small saucepan and bring to a boil. Reduce to a simmer for 5 minutes, or until you have a nice shiny glaze.

Us

½ cup (87 g) fresh pomegranate seeds, for serving

1. Uncover the rice and scoop it onto 2 plates. Top with the salmon, spooning the glaze over the top, and sprinkle over with the pomegranate seeds.

Thai Style Fish Cakes with Papaya Salad

If you add a bunch of amazing ingredients like these Thai influenced ones, blend them with a high-quality protein and pan-fry them in the shape of a patty, you can't lose. I LOVE these fish cakes, but I also really love the papaya salad with it. By making it in a classic style with a mortar and pestle you release the flavors and break down the vegetables into something that, after marinating in its dressing, is soft and intense. I don't have a large enough mortar, so I use the bottom of a heavy glass and a mixing bowl to crush up the ingredients for the salad. You need to put a little elbow grease in.

See recipe for one in the kitchen on page 197

For the Fish Cakes:

10 extra fine green beans

1 shoot lemongrass

3 scallions or spring onions

1 ½ tablespoons fish sauce

1 tablespoon Thai red curry paste

1 small handful of cilantro/coriander, plus more for serving

1 tablespoon sugar

2 limes

1 large egg

Two 8-ounce filets white fish (cod, haddock, whiting, or sole) (500 g)

2 tablespoons breadcrumbs

1 teaspoon salt

3 tablespoons olive oil

For the Salad:

2 handfuls (100 g) of extra fine green beans

1 to 2 red bird's eye chilis (depending on your heat preference)

1 small garlic clove

2 tablespoons sugar

4 cherry tomatoes

1 ½ tablespoons fish sauce

2 tablespoons fresh lime juice

1 carrot

1 small or 1/2 medium papaya

2 tablespoons peanuts

Ingredients

10 extra fine green beans

1 shoot lemongrass

3 scallions or spring onions

1 ½ tablespoons fish sauce

1 tablespoon Thai red curry paste

1 small handful of cilantro/coriander

1 tablespoon sugar

1 large egg

2 tablespoons breadcrumbs

1 teaspoon salt

2 tablespoons peanuts

3 tablespoons olive oil

You

1. Preheat the oven to 330°F (165°C).

2. Use scissors to cut the lemongrass, scallions, and green beans into smaller pieces.

3. In a blender or the bowl of a food processor, add the green beans, lemongrass, scallions, fish sauce, curry paste, cilantro, sugar, 2 tablespoons water, 1 tablespoon of the lime juice from ME, and the egg. Blend.

4. Add the diced fish from ME, the salt, and breadcrumbs. Blitz to a smooth paste.

5. Scoop this paste into 8 even balls and press down into burger-shaped patties. Place these in the fridge to chill for 5 minutes.

6. In a large ovenproof skillet over medium-high heat, add the peanuts and toast until starting to brown and giving off a nutty odour, 1 to 2 minutes. Remove and set aside.

7. Add the olive oil to the pan and add the fish cakes. Fry for 5 minutes on each side, then transfer to the oven to cook for 5 more minutes.

Ingredients

Me

2 limes

Two 8-ounce filets white fish (cod, haddock,
whiting, or sole) (500 g)

1 carrot

1 small or 1/2 medium papaya

1 small garlic clove

2 handfuls (100 g) of extra fine green beans

1 to 2 red bird's eye chilis (depending on your
heat preference)

2 tablespoons sugar

4 cherry tomatoes

2 tablespoons fish sauce

1. Cut the limes in half and juice them into a small
    bowl. This will be divided between the fish cakes
    and the salad dressing. Pass 1 tablespoon of the
    lime juice to YOU.

2. Remove the skin from the fish (if there is any) and
    cut it into cubes and pass to YOU.

3. Grate the carrot. Set aside.

4. Remove the seeds from the papaya with a spoon.
    If using a green papaya, peel and grate it as well.
    If you are using a ripe one, cut the flesh away from
    the skin and cut it into bite-size pieces. Set aside.

5. Halve the garlic clove. Trim the ends off the green
    beans. Remove the stems from the chilis.

6. In a mortar and pestle, add the green beans,
    chilis, garlic, and sugar. Pound to combine. If you
    don't have a mortar and pestle, you can place the
    ingredients in a medium bowl and use the edge of
    a heavy glass to crush them.

7. Add the tomatoes and crush for a final time.

8. Add 2 tablespoons fish sauce and the rest of the
    lime juice. Add the carrot and papaya. Toss to
    combine and let marinate for 5 minutes.

See next page for us directions.

Ingredients

Fresh cilantro/coriander

1 red chili, sliced

Us

1. Divide the salad between 2 plates and serve with the fish cakes on top. Garnish with the toasted peanuts from YOU, the cilantro, and sliced chilis.

Thai Style Fish Cakes with Papaya Salad

Chapter Four:

Poultry and Meat

The Healthiest Chicken Caesar Salad

This is a great recipe to start with for novice cooks. It's super simple and requires almost no chopping. It comes together in about 20 minutes and makes a fresh, healthy dinner or lunch. As you get more comfortable cooking together, you can add more elements like cooked bacon, sliced radishes, boiled eggs, etc. Massaging the kale is key to getting it nice and soft. Don't skip this step! I recommend making the full amount of dressing but using only half to start. Everyone has different preferences when it comes to dressing a salad, and a creamy dressing like this can be even more overpowering, so start small and add more.

See recipe for one in the kitchen on page 198

For the Chicken Salad:

1 large bunch of curly or lacinato/Cavolo

Nero kale

1 tablespoon plus 1 teaspoon olive oil

¾ teaspoon salt

Two 6-ounce chicken breasts (340 g)

1 teaspoon paprika

½ cup (70 g) unsalted, raw cashews

2 ripe avocados

Freshly ground black pepper, for serving

2 tablespoons (11 g) grated Parmesan

cheese, for serving

For the Dressing:

2 anchovy filets

1 garlic clove

Juice of ½ lemon

2 tablespoons olive oil

2 teaspoons soy sauce

2 tablespoons (11 g) grated Parmesan cheese

1/3 cup (85 g) plain Greek yogurt

Salt and freshly ground black pepper, to taste

Ingredients

You

Two 6-ounce chicken breasts (340 g)

1 teaspoon paprika

½ teaspoon salt

1 tablespoon olive oil

½ cup (70 g) unsalted, raw cashews

2 ripe avocados

1. Preheat the oven to 400°F (200°C).

2. Pat the chicken breasts dry with paper towels and season by rubbing the paprika and salt evenly over them.

3. In an ovenproof frying pan over high heat, heat the olive oil until it sizzles. Add the chicken breasts. Cook until browned, 1 to 2 minutes per side, then transfer to the oven to cook the chicken for another 10 minutes. Remove from the oven and allow the chicken to rest in the pan for another 10 minutes.

4. In a small pan over medium heat, add the cashews and toast until browned and giving off a nice, nutty smell, 3 to 5 minutes. Transfer to a cutting board and crush with the back of a spoon.

5. Pit the avocados and scoop out the flesh. Cut into bite-size pieces. Divide the avocados between 2 medium bowls.

Ingredients

1 large bunch of curly or lacinato/Cavolo Nero kale

2 tablespoons plus 1 teaspoon olive oil

¼ teaspoon salt, plus more to taste

2 anchovy filets

1 garlic clove

Juice of ½ lemon

2 teaspoons soy sauce

2 tablespoons (11 g) grated Parmesan cheese

1/3 cup (85 g) plain Greek yogurt

Freshly ground black pepper, to taste

Me

1. Tear the kale away from its stem and into small, bite-size pieces. Rinse well. In a large bowl, add the kale, 1 teaspoon of the olive oil, and ¼ teaspoon of the salt. Massage the kale for 2 minutes. Set aside.

2. Make the dressing: In a medium bowl, mash the anchovy filets against the side of a bowl with a fork, breaking them down.

3. Grate the garlic into the same bowl.

4. Add the lemon juice, the remaining 2 tablespoons olive oil, the soy sauce, grated cheese, and Greek yogurt. Mix well to combine. Add salt and black pepper to taste.

Us

Freshly ground black pepper

2 tablespoons (11 g) grated Parmesan cheese

1. When the chicken has rested for 10 minutes, thinly slice it against the grain of the meat.

2. Divide the kale, cashews, and half of the dressing to the bowls with the avocado.

3. Toss to combine everything and taste. Add more dressing to your preference.

4. Top the salads with the chicken. Serve with more grated cheese and more black pepper.

The Healthiest Chicken Caesar Salad

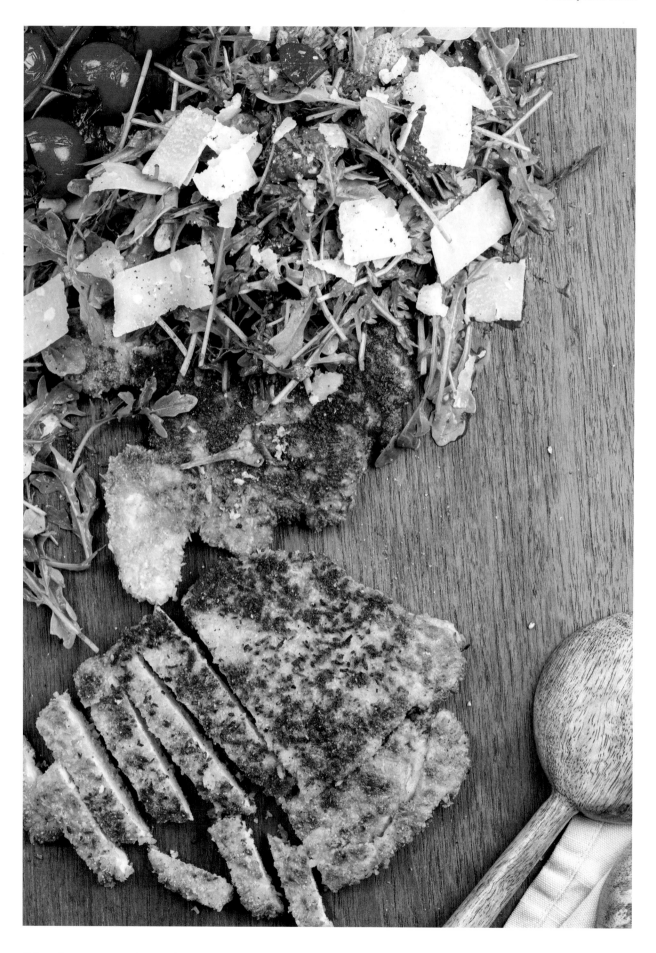

Crispy Coconut and Almond Chicken with Roasted Tomato & Arugula Salad

Crispy Coconut and Almond Chicken with Roasted Tomato & Arugula Salad

This is the chicken recipe that I get asked for again and again; it's a healthy throwback to childhood, and honestly, it just makes everyone happy. By combining the nutty flavor of almonds with the tropical taste of coconut, you have a protein-rich dish that doesn't sacrifice the crispy coating for your chicken. I particularly love this as a recipe split for two, because it's so much easier to coat the chicken with four hands. The tomatoes roasted in olive oil burst beautifully, creating a tomato dressing for your salad.

See recipe for one in the kitchen on page 199

For the Chicken:

Two 6-ounce chicken breasts (340 g)

½ cup (60 g) almond flour

½ cup (45 g) shredded, unsweetened coconut

1 teaspoon paprika

¼ teaspoon salt

¼ teaspoon freshly ground black pepper

¾ cup (90 g) all-purpose or gluten-free flour

1 large egg

Splash of milk of choice

2 tablespoons unsalted butter

2 tablespoons vegetable oil

For the Salad:

4 cups (100 g) arugula/rocket

1 small handful of fresh cilantro/coriander leaves

Parmesan cheese shavings (optional)

Pinch of salt

For the Roasted Tomatoes:

6 ounces (170 g) cherry tomatoes

¼ tablespoon olive oil

Ingredients

6 ounces (170 g) cherry tomatoes

¼ tablespoon olive oil

½ cup (60 g) almond flour

½ cup (45 g) shredded, unsweetened coconut

1 teaspoon paprika

¼ teaspoon salt

¼ teaspoon freshly ground black pepper

¾ cup (90 g) all-purpose or gluten-free flour

1 large egg

Splash of milk of choice

1 small handful of fresh cilantro/coriander leaves

You

1.   Preheat the oven to 400°F (200°C).

2.   Toss the cherry tomatoes with the olive oil on a small baking sheet and roast for 10 minutes.

3.   Prepare 2 plates for breading the chicken: On one, whisk together the almond flour, coconut, paprika, 1/8 teaspoon of salt, and the pepper.

4.   On the second plate, whisk together the flour and the remaining 1/8 teaspoon salt.

5.   In a shallow bowl, whisk the egg with your milk of choice.

6.   Roughly chop the cilantro and set aside.

Ingredients

Me

Two 6-ounce chicken breasts (340 g)

1. Place the chicken breasts between 2 pieces of parchment paper and using a meat mallet, rolling pin, or wine or water bottle, gently pound them out to ¾-inch (2-centimeter) thickness.

Us

2 tablespoons unsalted butter

2 tablespoons vegetable oil

4 cups (100 g) arugula/rocket

Parmesan cheese shavings (optional)

Pinch of salt

1. Dip the flattened chicken first into the flour, shaking to remove excess, then into the egg and then finally into the almond and coconut, coating evenly.

2. In a large skillet or cast-iron pan over medium-high heat, melt the butter and vegetable oil.

3. Place one chicken breast in the pan and cook for 5 minutes on each side. Repeat with the second flattened chicken.

4. Toss the roasted tomatoes with the arugula, cilantro, shaved Parmesan, and salt.

5. Serve the chicken with the salad and roasted tomatoes.

Korean-Style Pork Noodles and Pickled Cucumber

Korean-Style Pork Noodles and Pickled Cucumber

This quick pork recipe is a variation on one that my mom introduced me to. Gochujang is a popular fermented chili paste that is widely used in Korean cuisine. It is made from chilis, rice, and fermented soybeans. It's very umami and really elevates this recipe but it can be hard to find. I order it online, but you can find it in some grocery stores. If you are struggling to find it, you can substitute chili garlic paste which is easier to find. One of the best parts of Korean cuisine is all the pickled condiments and I love the freshness of the quick-pickled cucumbers with this.

See recipe for one in the kitchen on page 200

For the Noodles:

2 tablespoons gochujang (or chili garlic paste)

1 tablespoon soy sauce

1 tablespoon sugar

1 finger-size piece of fresh ginger

3 ½ ounces (100 g) uncooked rice noodles

2 tablespoons olive oil

1 large onion

1 red bell pepper

2 garlic cloves

½ pound (250 g) ground pork

1 bunch of spring greens, collard greens, Chinese cabbage, or kale

2 scallions or spring onions, for serving

For the Cucumbers:

1 tablespoon rice vinegar

1 teaspoon sugar

½ teaspoon salt

½ large or 1 small cucumber

1 teaspoon sesame seeds

Ingredients

You

2 tablespoons gochujang
(or chili garlic paste)

1 tablespoon soy sauce

1 tablespoon sugar

1 finger-size piece of fresh ginger

3 ½ ounces (100 g) uncooked
rice noodles

2 tablespoons olive oil

½ pound (250g) ground pork

1. In a small bowl, whisk together the gochujang, soy sauce, sugar, and 1 cup (240 ml) water. Grate the ginger into it.

2. Cook the rice noodles according to the package instructions, then run under cold water to stop the cooking.

3. In a large skillet over medium-high heat, heat 1 tablespoon of the olive oil and add the onion, bell pepper, and garlic from ME. Cook until starting to brown and soften, about 10 minutes.

4. Remove the cooked vegetables from the pan. Add the remaining 1 tablespoon olive oil and the pork, breaking the meat up until it's brown and cooked through, 7 minutes.

5. Return the vegetables to the pan, along with the sliced greens from ME. Add the gochujang sauce. Bring to a boil.

6. Add the cooked noodles, tossing to combine.

Ingredients

1 large onion

1 red bell pepper

2 garlic cloves

1 bunch of spring greens, collard greens, Chinese cabbage, or kale

1 tablespoon rice vinegar

1 teaspoon sugar

½ teaspoon salt

½ large or 1 small cucumber

1 teaspoon sesame seeds

2 scallions or spring onions

Me

1. Finely chop the onion, bell pepper, and garlic. Pass to YOU.

2. Rinse and thinly slice the greens. Pass to YOU.

3. In a medium bowl, whisk together the rice vinegar, sugar, and salt.

4. Halve the cucumber lengthwise and use a spoon to scoop the seeds out. Thinly slice the remaining flesh of the cucumber and toss it in the rice vinegar mixture.

5. Add the sesame seeds. Set aside to marinate.

6. Thinly slice the scallions. Set aside.

Us

1. Spoon the noodle mixture into bowls and top with the pickled cucumber and scallions.

Lamb and Pistachio Kofta Salad

I used to work for a family that couldn't get enough lamb kofta. I have probably made 25 different versions of this dish, but it wasn't until I came across one that included pistachios in the kofta mix that I really loved them myself. I could eat pistachios in anything. They add a decadent richness to these flavorful little sausages. You'll need to get your hands dirty here rolling the koftas to shape so that they cook evenly. I love the simplicity of the tzatziki and Greek salad, and they are much improved if you use high-quality ingredients like 5% fat Greek yogurt and heirloom tomatoes.

See recipe for one in the kitchen on page 201

For the Koftas:

1 shallot

¼ cup (30 g) shelled pistachios

4 sprigs of mint, including stems

Zest of 1 lemon

1 tablespoon ground cumin

½ tablespoon chilli powder

1 teaspoon salt

½ pound (250 g) lamb mince

2 teaspoons olive oil

2 pita breads

For the Tzatziki:

¼ large cucumber

1 medium garlic clove

¾ cup (175 g) plain Greek yogurt

½ lemon

½ teaspoon fine sea salt

For the Salad:

2 medium heirloom tomatoes

¾ large cucumber

1 small red onion

2 teaspoons olive oil

1 teaspoon sherry vinegar

3 ½ ounces (100 g) feta cheese

Freshly ground black pepper

Ingredients

1 shallot

¼ cup (30 g) shelled pistachios

4 sprigs of mint, including stems

Zest of 1 lemon

1 tablespoon ground cumin

½ tablespoon chilli powder

1 teaspoon salt

½ pound (250 g) lamb mince

2 teaspoons olive oil

2 pita breads

You

1.   Preheat the oven to the Broil/Grill setting at 450°F (230°C).

2.   Peel the shallot. In a blender or the bowl of a food processor, add the shallot, pistachios, mint, lemon zest, cumin, chili powder, and salt. Blitz until the ingredients are fine and blended. Add the lamb and pulse for another 30 seconds until just combined.

3.   Form the meat into 6 equal portions and roll each one into a cylindrical or oval shape, ensuring that they are evenly formed. Lightly drizzle the oil over the kebabs and use your hands to roll them in it, ensuring an even coating.

4.   Place the koftas on a grill-safe tray under the broiler/grill, turning every few minutes until all sides are evenly cooked to golden brown. Remove and allow to cool.

5.   Turn off the broiler/grill and toss the pita breads into the hot oven for 1 minute to warm slightly.

Ingredients

1 large cucumber

1 medium garlic clove

¾ cup (175 g) plain Greek yogurt

½ lemon

 Fine sea salt

2 medium heirloom tomatoes

¾ large cucumber, halved lengthwise and sliced into half moons

1 small red onion

2 teaspoons olive oil

1 teaspoon sherry vinegar

Freshly ground black pepper

3 ½ ounces (100 g) feta cheese

Me

1. Make the tzatziki: In a medium bowl, grate in 1/4 cucumber and the garlic. Add the Greek yogurt, lemon juice, and ½ teaspoon of salt. Stir to combine.

2. Make the salad: Slice the tomatoes and arrange on a plate.

3. Halve the remaining ¾ cucumber lengthwise and slice into half-moons. Add to a large bowl.

4. Thinly slice the red onion and add it to the cucumber in the bowl. Toss with the olive oil and vinegar and add salt and pepper to taste.

5. Spread this cucumber and onion mix on top of the sliced tomatoes and crumble the feta over the top.

6. Crack black pepper over the salad.

Us

1. Top the salad with the kofta and tzatziki. Serve with the warm pita on the side.

Lamb and Pistachio Kofta Salad

Mediterranean Quinoa with Blackened Chicken

Mediterranean Quinoa with Blackened Chicken

Louisiana-style blackened chicken is a popular and flavorful dish that originated in the Cajun and Creole cuisines of the Pelican State. It takes simple yet delicious preparation that involves coating chicken breasts in a blend of spices and herbs and then searing them in a cast-iron skillet until they are charred on the outside and tender and juicy on the inside. The robust flavor of the chicken pairs well with the light, acidic quinoa salad and makes a perfect summery lunch or dinner.

See recipe for one in the kitchen on page 202

For the Chicken & Quinoa:

2 teaspoons salt

1 ½ teaspoons garlic powder

1 teaspoon ground white pepper

1 teaspoon onion powder

1 teaspoon chili powder

1 teaspoon dried oregano

1 teaspoon dried thyme

1 teaspoon smoked paprika

Two 6-ounce boneless, skinless chicken breasts (340 g)

5 tablespoons olive oil

½ cup (70 g) pumpkin seeds

½ cup uncooked quinoa

For the Salad:

1 cup arugula/rocket

½ cucumber

¾ cup (110 g) cherry tomatoes

½ cup (100 g) feta cheese

1 shallot

1 handful of fresh basil

½ cup raw, unsalted cashews

Juice of 1 lemon

1 tablespoon honey

1 garlic clove

½ teaspoon salt

Ingredients

You

½ cup raw, unsalted cashews

2 teaspoons salt

1 ½ teaspoons garlic powder

1 teaspoon ground white pepper

1 teaspoon onion powder

1 teaspoon chili powder

1 teaspoon dried oregano

1 teaspoon dried thyme

1 teaspoon smoked paprika

Two 6-ounce boneless, skinless chicken breasts (340 g)

2 1/2 tablespoons olive oil

1. Preheat the oven to 400°F (200°C).

2. Add the cashews to a small bowl and cover with boiling water. Let soak for 15 minutes, until softened. Drain. Pass to ME.

3. In a large shallow bowl, whisk together the salt, garlic powder, white pepper, onion powder, chili powder, oregano, thyme, and paprika.

4. Dredge the chicken in the spice mix so they are thoroughly coated.

5. In an ovenproof frying pan or cast-iron skillet over medium heat, heat ½ tablespoon of the olive oil. Add the pumpkin seeds, toasting until they start to brown and make a popping noise, about 2 minutes. Remove them from the pan.

6. Add the remaining 2 tablespoons olive oil to the pan and increase the heat slightly. Add the chicken breasts and cook until the spice mixture is turning black and forming a crust around the chicken, 2 minutes per side. Transfer the pan to the oven and bake for 8 minutes. Remove the chicken from the oven, place on a cutting board, and allow to rest for 10 minutes.

Ingredients

Me

½ cup (70 g) pumpkin seeds

½ cup uncooked quinoa

½ cucumber

¾ cup (110 g) cherry tomatoes

½ cup (100 g) feta cheese

1 shallot

1 cup arugula/rocket

1 handful of fresh basil

Juice of 1 lemon

1 tablespoon honey

1 garlic clove

½ teaspoon salt

1. In a fine-mesh sieve, rinse the quinoa under running water briefly.

2. In a large skillet or shallow pot with a lid, add the quinoa and 1 cup (230 ml) water. Bring to a boil. Reduce to a simmer and cook, covered, until the liquid has been absorbed and the quinoa is tender, another 10 to 15 minutes. Remove from the heat and allow to rest, covered.

3. Dice the cucumber and feta. Quarter the cherry tomatoes. Finely chop the shallot. Add to a large bowl. Add the arugula.

4. Separate the leaves from the stems of the basil. Reserve the stems. Chop the leaves.

5. Add half of the chopped basil leaves to the bowl with the arugula and vegetables.

6. In a blender or the bowl of a food processor, add the soaked cashews from YOU, ½ cup water, the basil stems, the remaining half of the basil leaves, the lemon juice, honey, garlic, and salt. Blend to form a dressing.

7. Once the quinoa has rested for 5 minutes, toss it through the vegetables and add the toasted pumpkin seeds.

See next page for us directions.

Us

1. Slice the rested blackened chicken against the grain.

2. Pour the dressing over the quinoa and salad.

3. Spoon the quinoa salad onto 2 plates and top with the blackened chicken.

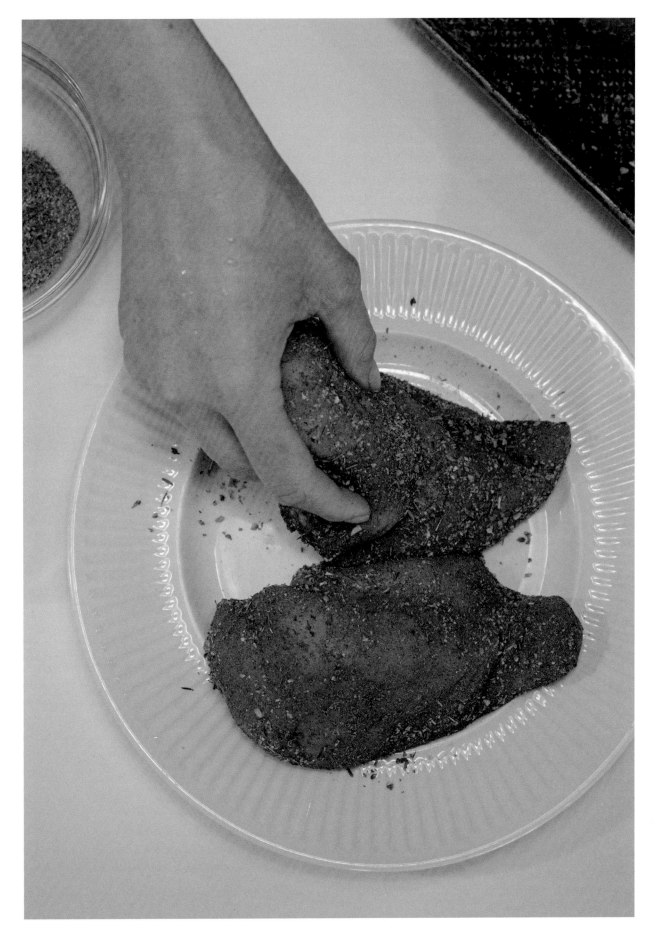

Mediterranean Quinoa with Blackened Chicken

Chicken Pozole Stew

Usually made with pork, my pozole – or spicy Mexican hominy stew – is made with chicken thighs. They cook faster, so a typically three-hour dish can come together in half the time here with the same delicious rich flavors as the traditional version. Hominy is a type of corn kernel specific to Mexican cuisine. If you can't find it at your grocery store, you can buy it canned at Mexican shops or online. Like any braised dish, this will need some cooking time, but the down time is a great opportunity to get the clean-up done and the garnishes prepped. The addition of chicken wings/bones adds a richness to the soup base and should be cheap to buy. Just be sure to discard the bones before serving! Serve the stew with a dollop of yogurt if it's a bit too hot for your taste.

See recipe for one in the kitchen on page 203

Ingredients:

2 tablespoons olive oil

1 pound (500 g) chicken wings or bones

Salt

1 ½ pounds (700 g) bone-in chicken thighs

6 garlic cloves

1 yellow onion

1 tablespoon dried oregano

½ teaspoon ground cumin

4 cups (1 liter) chicken stock

1 dried bay leaf

4 to 6 dried guajillo or ancho chiles (depending on your heat preference)

One 28-ounce (822 g) can white hominy

1 tablespoon apple cider vinegar

For Serving:

¼ small cabbage

½ bunch of fresh cilantro/coriander

1 handful of red radishes

1 avocado

1 lime

1 cup corn chips (optional)

Dollop of plain Greek yogurt (optional)

Ingredients

You

2 tablespoons olive oil

1 pound (500 g) chicken wings or bones

Salt

1 ½ pounds (700 g) bone-in chicken thighs

1 tablespoon dried oregano

1/2 teaspoon ground cumin

4 cups (1 liter) chicken stock

1 dried bay leaf

One 28-ounce (822 g) can white hominy

1. In a deep, heavy-bottomed pot over high heat, heat the olive oil. Add the chicken wings and a large pinch of salt and cook, tossing every so often, until thoroughly browned. Remove from the pan and set aside.

2. Remove the skin from the chicken thighs and season generously with salt.

3. Add the chicken thighs to the pan, browning both sides, about 2 minutes per side.

4. Remove the chicken thighs from the pan and add the onion and chopped garlic from ME along with the cumin and oregano. Cook for 3 minutes.

5. Add the chicken thighs and wings back in and cover with the chicken stock and 1 cup (240 ml) water. Add the bay leaf. Scrape any bits that stick to the bottom of the pan.

6. Bring to a boil, then reduce the heat to medium-low and cook until the chicken thighs are tender, about 45 minutes. Skim any foam or oil off the surface as it cooks.

7. Drain and rinse the hominy.

Ingredients

4 to 6 dried guajillo or ancho chiles (depending on your heat preference)

6 garlic cloves

1 yellow onion

1/4 small cabbage

1 handful of red radishes

1/2 bunch of fresh cilantro/coriander

1 avocado

1 lime

Me

1. In a small pan, bring water to a boil. Add the chilis, reduce the heat to low, and cook until soft, 10 minutes. Reserve 1 cup of the cooking water. Drain the chilis.

2. Chop 3 of the garlic cloves and leave the remaining 3 whole. Pass the chopped garlic to YOU.

3. Quarter the yellow onion and pass to YOU.

4. In a blender, add the softened chilis, the whole garlic, and the reserved cooking water. Blend and set aside.

5. Prepare the garnishes: Thinly slice the cabbage and radishes. Chop the cilantro. Pit the avocado. Scoop out the flesh and slice it. Halve the lime.

See next page for us directions.

Ingredients

1 tablespoon apple cider vinegar

1 cup corn chips (optional)

Dollop of plain Greek yogurt (optional)

Us

1. Remove all the meat and the onion quarters from the soup, separating out the thighs from the rest. Pull the meat off the thighs.

2. Pour half of the chili blend into the remaining liquid. Add the hominy and vinegar. Bring to a boil.

3. Taste the broth and if you want more spice, add the remaining chili mixture.

4. Return the pulled chicken meat to the soup and cook all together for 10 more minutes.

5. Spoon the soup into 2 bowls and garnish liberally with the cabbage, cilantro, radishes, avocado, lime, and corn chips (if using). Add a dollop of yogurt (if using).

Chopped Salad, Beverly Hills Style

This is the recipe that I think best showcases the wonders of a tandem cooking style. While this salad is incredibly delicious, it does require a fair amount of preparation. The key to its great taste lies in the chopping technique, which is why—go figure—it's called a "chopped" salad. A small dice here works best, but the main thing is that everything is consistently sized so the flavors balance perfectly together. This version of a chopped salad originated in the Polo Lounge of the Beverly Hills Hotel and has since been adapted by many restaurants worldwide before finally being served up to you here as a great recipe for team cooking.

See recipe for one in the kitchen on page 204

For the Salad:

2 large eggs

5 slices/rashers of streaky bacon

One 6-ounce chicken breast (170 g)

2 whole, unpeeled garlic cloves

¼ cup (115 g) balsamic vinegar

1 shallot

½ tablespoon brown sugar

½ teaspoon Dijon mustard

Salt and freshly ground black pepper, to taste

½ cup olive oil

1 large head romaine lettuce

1 cup (100 g) cherry tomatoes

1 ripe avocado

1 cup (120 g) aged cheddar cheese

2 cooked and peeled beets

Ingredients

You

2 large eggs

5 slices/rashers of streaky bacon

One 6-ounce chicken breast (170 g)

2 unpeeled garlic cloves

¼ cup (115 g) balsamic vinegar

½ tablespoon brown sugar

½ teaspoon Dijon mustard

Salt and freshly ground black pepper, to taste

½ cup olive oil

1. Preheat the oven to 400ºF (200ºC).

2. Boil a small pot of water. Add the eggs and cook for 10 minutes. Remove and drain in a colander, running cold water over them until they are cool enough to touch. Pass to ME.

3. Line a plate with paper towels.

4. In a large ovenproof frying pan over medium heat, add the bacon. Cook, turning once, until crispy. Keeping the bacon fat in the pan, remove the bacon and drain on the prepared plate. Pass the bacon to ME.

5. In the same pan over medium-high heat, add the chicken breast. Sear both sides in the bacon fat until browned but not cooked through, 1 minute per side.

6. Add the unpeeled garlic to the pan with the chicken. Transfer to the oven and cook for 10 minutes. Remove and allow to cool. Pass to ME.

Ingredients

Me

1 shallot

1 large head romaine lettuce

1 cup (100 g) cherry tomatoes

1 ripe avocado

1 cup (120 g) aged cheddar cheese

2 cooked and peeled beets

1. Finely dice the shallot and set aside for later.

2. Remove any wilted or damaged outer leaves from the head of lettuce and discard them. Cut off the end of the lettuce where the stem was attached and discard it. Starting at the head of the lettuce, slice the lettuce horizontally into thin ribbons. Set aside.

3. Quarter the cherry tomatoes and set aside.

4. Pit the avocado and use a spoon to scoop out the flesh. Cut it into ½-inch (1-centimeter) cubes. Set aside.

5. Cut the beets and cheddar into ½-inch (1-centimeter) cubes.

6. Peel and cut the hard-boiled eggs from YOU into a rough dice.

7. Finely chop the cooked, cooled bacon from YOU.

8. Remove the garlic cloves from YOU from their skin and crush with the side of a knife. Chop.

9. In a small bowl, whisk together the garlic, balsamic vinegar, shallot, brown sugar, Dijon mustard, salt, and pepper. Slowly drizzle in the olive oil as you whisk, emulsifying slowly until you have a thick, creamy dressing.

10. Cut the cooked chicken from YOU into ½-inch (1-centimeter) cubes.

See next page for us directions.

Chopped Salad, Beverly Hills Style

Us

1. To assemble the salad, layer the shredded lettuce on the bottom of 2 bowls and divide the eggs, bacon, tomatoes, avocado, cheese cubes, and beets between the bowls. Toss with the dressing.

Chopped Salad, Beverly Hills Style

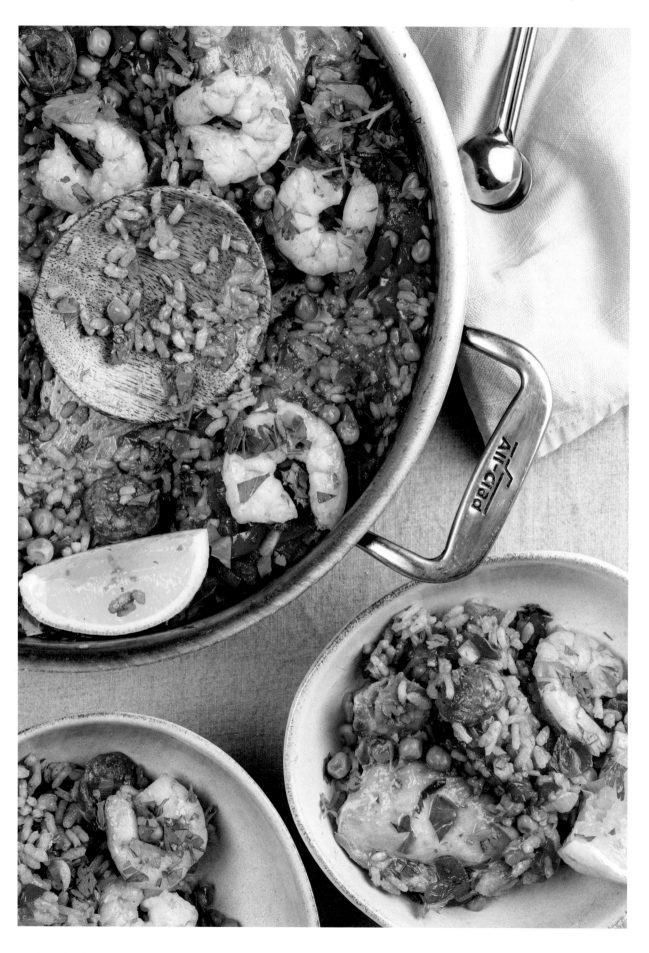

Perfect Paella

Paella has evolved into a symbol of celebration and togetherness in Spain where it originates from. It brings people from all walks of life together around its rich flavors to bask in the joy of shared company. Because of that, it suits the ethos of Cook Together perfectly. It's also a straightforward dish that comes together quickly with ME doing the chopping and measuring and YOU getting everything in the pan and cooking. Remember not to stir it once the broth is in. You want a lovely crust to form on the bottom of the pan, traditionally called the socarrat. If you are using an induction stovetop/hob, be sure to move the pan around so that the rice cooks evenly and not just in the middle.

See recipe for one in the kitchen on page 205

Ingredients

Two 6-ounce boneless, skinless chicken thighs (340 g)

¼ teaspoon salt, plus more as needed

5 ounces (140 g) cooking chorizo

Olive oil, as needed

1 onion

1 red bell pepper

2 garlic cloves

2 medium tomatoes

1 teaspoon paprika

1 pinch saffron threads

¼ cup white wine

1 cup (200 g) Spanish or medium-grain rice

2 cups (475 ml) chicken broth

1 dried bay leaf

About 12 jumbo shrimp or prawns, tail on and peeled

½ cup (75 g) frozen peas, thawed

1 handful of fresh parsley

1 lemon

Ingredients

You

Two 6-ounce boneless, skinless chicken thighs (340 g)

¼ teaspoon salt, plus more as needed

Olive oil, as needed

1. Season the chicken well with salt.

2. Line a plate with paper towels. Set aside.

3. In a medium frying pan with a lid over high heat, add the chorizo rounds from ME. Cook on high until browning. Keeping the grease in the pan, remove the chorizo with a slotted spoon and transfer to the prepared plate.

4. Add the chicken thighs. Sear until browned and released from the pan, about 2 minutes. Flip and cook for another 2 minutes. Remove from the pan.

5. Add olive oil to the pan if needed. Add the chopped onion, bell pepper, and garlic from ME. Reduce the heat slightly and cook for 5 minutes until softened. Scrape to get any chicken bits off the bottom of the pan.

6. Add the chopped tomato and paprika mixture from ME and cook on medium-high until the tomatoes are breaking down and the liquid is evaporated, about 5 minutes more.

7. Add the wine and saffron from ME and cook until reduced by half. Season with salt if needed.

8. Add the rice, stirring to ensure even coverage. Nestle the chicken thighs and chorizo back in.

9. Evenly pour the broth over the top, ensuring all the rice and chicken is covered. Add the bay leaf. Bring the mixture to a boil, then reduce the heat to medium-low. Stir once after it's boiled to distribute the heat around the pan.

Ingredients

5 ounces (140 g) cooking chorizo,

sliced into rounds

1 onion

1 red bell pepper

2 garlic cloves

2 medium tomatoes

1/4 cup white wine

1 cup (200 g) Spanish or medium-grain rice

2 cups (475 ml) chicken broth

1 dried bay leaf

1 teaspoon paprika

1 pinch saffron threads

1 handful of fresh parsley

About 12 jumbo shrimp or prawns, tail on and

peeled

1/2 cup (75 g) frozen peas, thawed

1 lemon

Me

1. Slice the chorizo into thin rounds. Pass to YOU.

2. Dice the onion, bell pepper, and garlic. Pass to YOU.

3. Very finely chop the tomato, combine it with the paprika, and pass to YOU.

4. Combine the wine with the saffron. Pass to YOU.

5. Measure the chicken broth and the rice separately. Pass to YOU.

6. Finely chop the parsley.

7. Measure out the peas and shrimp.

8. Rinse the shrimp/prawns under running water.

9. Slice the lemon into wedges.

Us

1. Cook for about 20 minutes. Don't stir (this allows a crust to form on the bottom of the pan).

2. Add the shrimp and peas to the top of the mixture. Cook for another 5 minutes. Add a bit of water if your rice isn't cooked through fully.

3. Place a lid or foil over the dish and remove it from the heat, allowing it to steam for 10 minutes.

4. Sprinkle the parsley over the top and serve with lemon wedges!

Chicken Biryani

A dish like biryani must be enjoyed with good company, and this recipe is the perfect introduction to this gorgeous Indian favorite. The blend of warming spices like clove and star-anise partnered with the chicken marinated in cool yogurt and acidic tomato make this a perfect one-pot dish. Most Indian cuisine requires quite a few spices and I've stuck with traditional ingredients here so you can get the authentic feeling from the dish. I believe these are all great pantry staple spices to have on hand and you'll see them come up throughout the rest of this book. If you can't find one or two, don't worry too much, you can omit them. This dish is hard to mess up with all the delicious flavors going on.

See recipe for one in the kitchen on page 206

For the Biryani:

1 pound (400 g) boneless, skinless chicken thighs

4 tablespoons vegetable oil

2 medium yellow onions

Salt

2 tablespoons whole milk

1 ½ tablespoons unsalted butter

1 teaspoon saffron threads

5 whole cloves

1 dried bay leaf

1 star anise

3 green cardamon pods

1 cup (225 g) uncooked basmati rice

1 cup fresh cilantro/coriander leaves

1 cup fresh mint leaves

½ cup plain Greek yogurt, plus more for serving

For the Marinade:

½ cup (37 ml) plain Greek yogurt

¼ cup tomato paste

2 tablespoons olive oil

3 garlic cloves

1-inch piece of fresh ginger

1 teaspoon ground turmeric

1 teaspoon garam masala

1 teaspoon salt

Ingredients

1 cup (74 ml) plain Greek yogurt

1/4 cup tomato paste

2 tablespoons olive oil

3 garlic cloves

1-inch piece of fresh ginger

1 teaspoon ground turmeric

1 teaspoon garam masala

Salt

1 pound (400 g) boneless,
skinless chicken thighs

4 tablespoons vegetable oil

You

1. Make the marinade by combining ½ cup yoghurt, olive oil, peeled garlic cloves, ginger, turmeric, garam marsala, tomato paste and salt in a blender.

2. Toss chicken thighs to coat and place out of the way for 30mins.

3. Heat 4 tablespoon of oil in a hot pan and add the onion, sautéing until brown and sweet. Season with salt. Drain onto a paper towel and set aside.

4. While the onions are cooking combine the remaining ½ cup Greek yoghurt with a pinch of salt and ½ of the mint leaves prepared by ME. Place in the fridge to save for serving.

Ingredients

2 medium yellow onions

1 cup fresh cilantro/coriander leaves, roughly chopped

1 cup fresh mint leaves, roughly chopped

2 tablespoons whole milk

1 ½ tablespoons unsalted butter

1 teaspoon saffron threads

Salt

5 whole cloves

1 dried bay leaf

1 star anise

3 green cardamon pods

1 cup (225 g) uncooked basmati rice

Me

1. Thinly slice the onions. Pass these to YOU.

2. Chop the cilantro leaves roughly and add to a small bowl. Set aside.

3. Chop the mint leaves roughly and pass half to YOU. Add the other half to the bowl with the chopped cilantro.

4. In a small saucepan over medium heat, add the milk, butter, and saffron. Cook until the butter has melted, 2 minutes. Remove from the heat and let sit.

5. Bring a large pot of water to a boil and add ½ teaspoon of salt, the cloves, bay leaf, star anise, and cardamom pods. Allow to boil for 5 minutes.

6. Add the rice and allow to boil for 4 minutes. Drain and set aside.

See next page for us directions.

Ingredients

Dollop of plain Greek yogurt

Us

1. Remove the marinated chicken from the fridge. In a heavy-bottomed pot with a lid over medium heat, add the marinated chicken. Cook for 4 minutes, then turn the chicken pieces once. Cover with the lid and cook for another 3 minutes. Turn off the heat.

2. Scatter half of the browned onions all over the chicken. Sprinkle with the cilantro and ½ cup of the mint leaves.

3. Next layer the rice over the mint and cilantro. Drizzle the saffron milk and butter all over the rice.

4. Cover the pot with the lid and cook over low heat, 20 minutes. Remove from the heat and let rest for 5 to 10 minutes. Scatter the remaining onions on top.

5. In a medium bowl, combine the yogurt, the remaining ½ cup mint, and a pinch of salt.

6. Garnish the biryani with a dollop of the yogurt and the mint yogurt sauce.

Warm Steak Salad with Fried Artichokes

Warm Steak Salad with Fried Artichokes

Fried artichoke hearts are a secret weapon in any salad, or on their own. They pair wonderfully with this juicy steak and complement the sharp horseradish dressing you'll use for this salad. Make sure you watch them as you deep fry them, though; you'll know they are finished because their moisture will disappear and the leaves will start to fan outward. Use a high-quality steak here (you don't need much) and cook it for just a few minutes on high heat on each side.

See recipe for one in the kitchen on page 207

For the Pickled Onion:

½ red onion

¼ cup (60 ml) white wine vinegar

¼ cup (60 ml) water

1 tablespoon sugar

1 teaspoon salt

For the Dressing:

1 tablespoon horseradish (tinned or fresh)

1 tablespoon white wine vinegar

1 tablespoon honey

2 tablespoons olive oil

Salt and freshly ground black pepper, to taste

For the Steak Salad:

One 7-ounce (200-g) filet of beef (you can use sirloin if preferred)

Salt and freshly ground black pepper

12 ounces (350 g) new potatoes

½ cup (100 ml) sunflower or other high-heat oil

One 7-ounce (200-g) tin oil-packed artichoke hearts

½ cup (40 g) raw walnut halves

2 big handfuls of mixed salad leaves

Ingredients

One 7-ounce (200g) filet of beef (you can use sirloin if preferred)

¼ cup (60 ml) white wine vinegar

¼ cup (60 ml) water

1 tablespoon sugar

Salt and freshly ground black pepper

1 tablespoon horseradish (tinned or fresh)

1 tablespoon white wine vinegar

1 tablespoon honey

2 tablespoons olive oil

You

1. Pull your steak out of the fridge if you haven't already.

2. In a small saucepan, add the vinegar, ¼ cup water, the sugar, and 1 teaspoon salt. Bring to a boil.

3. Pour the mixture over the onion slices from ME. Let pickle for at least 10 minutes.

4. In a large bowl, whisk together the horseradish, honey, and white wine vinegar. Add the oil slowly and season with salt and pepper. Set the dressing aside.

5. Season your steak liberally with salt and pepper.

6. In a frying pan over high heat, heat 1 tablespoon oil. Add the steak and fry until you get a nice crispy outer shell on the filet, 2 to 3 minutes per side. Remove and let rest for 5 minutes.

Ingredients

½ red onion

12 ounces (350 g) new potatoes

Salt

One 7-ounce (200-g) tin oil-packed artichoke hearts

½ cup (100 ml) sunflower or other high-
heat oil

½ cup (40 g) raw walnut halves

Me

1. Preheat the oven to 350°F (180°C).

2. Thinly slice the onion and add to a heatproof
    bowl. Hand to YOU.

3. Halve the potatoes.

4. In a pot, add cold water (enough to cover the
    potatoes) and salt. Add the potatoes. Bring to a
    boil. Allow to cook until soft but not falling apart,
    about 10 minutes. Drain.

5. Line a plate with paper towels. Set aside.

6. Drain the artichokes.

7. In a small saucepan over high heat, heat the
    sunflower oil. Fry the drained artichokes in the
    hot oil until crispy. You can tell that they are fin-
    ished when they start fanning out and air bub-
    bles stop rising to the surface, 6 to 8 minutes.
    Remove them with a slotted spoon and transfer
    to the prepared plate. Season them with salt.

8. Put the walnut halves on a baking sheet and
    toast in the oven for 5 minutes, or until starting
    to brown and smell nutty.

See next page for us directions.

Ingredients

2 big handfuls of mixed salad leaves

Us

1. In the bowl with the dressing, add the potatoes, salad leaves, artichoke hearts, and walnuts and toss. Serve on 2 plates.

2. Slice the steak and top each salad with it. Top with the pickled onions.

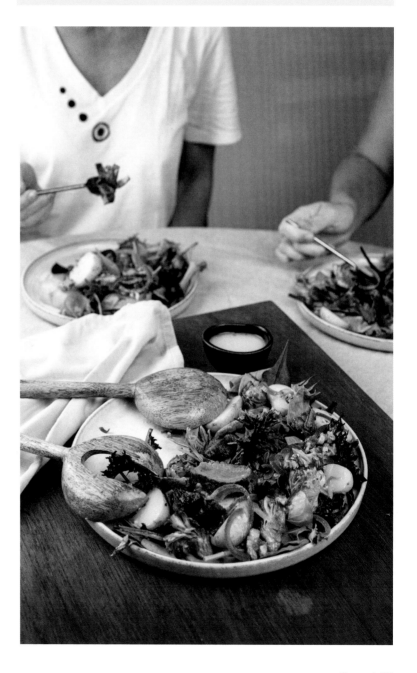

APPENDIX I:

Recipe Files for One in the Kitchen

For those solo nights, here is each recipe from the book
tailor-made for one cook only.

Lentil Dhal with Speedy Dosas

For the Dhal:

1 medium tomato

1 small bunch of fresh cilantro/coriander (about 1 cup)

3 garlic cloves

1 thumb-size piece of fresh ginger

1 tablespoon olive oil

1 small red onion, thinly sliced

1 to 2 red chilis (depending on your heat preference), thinly sliced

5 dried curry leaves

1 teaspoon ground turmeric

½ teaspoon ground cumin

½ teaspoon fenugreek seeds

One 14-ounce (400 g) can full-fat coconut milk

¾ cup (150 g) red split lentils

¼ teaspoon salt

For the Dosas:

1 large egg, beaten

½ cup plus 1 tablespoon (150 ml) milk

¾ cup (100 g) buckwheat flour

1 tablespoon melted unsalted butter

¼ teaspoon sea or kosher salt

Olive oil

For Serving:

½ cup plain yogurt (you can also use coconut yogurt), for serving

1. Make the dhal: In a food processor or blender, place the tomato, ¾ cup of the cilantro (including the stems), the garlic, and ginger with ¼ cup (60 ml) water. Blend and set aside.

2. In a large pot over medium heat, heat the olive oil and add the onion and chilis. Cook until translucent, 5 to 7 minutes.

3. Add the curry leaves, turmeric, cumin, and fenugreek seeds and cook for 1 minute more.

4. Add the blended tomato mixture and turn the heat up slightly.

5. Reduce until the liquid is absorbed.

6. Add the coconut milk, lentils, salt, and ¾ cup (175 ml) water.

7. Bring to a boil. Put a lid on and reduce to a simmer, stirring regularly, until the lentils are soft, about 20 minutes.

8. Make the dosas: In a bowl, add the egg, milk, ½ cup plus 1 tablespoon (150 ml) water, the buckwheat flour, butter, and salt to make a batter that's like a crepe batter, i.e., slightly runnier than a regular pancake batter. Add more water if needed.

9. Heat a nonstick skillet or crepe pan over high heat. Wait until the pan is very hot and add a little bit of oil. Ladle a scoop of the batter into the pan. Use the handle of the pan to swirl the batter around the pan into a thin layer. It should start to bubble immediately.

10. Drizzle 1 teaspoon olive oil around the edge of each dosa so it crisps up.

11. When the bottom turns dark gold-brown and the edges are crispy, flip the dosa over. Cook another 30 seconds and transfer to a plate.

12. Repeat with the rest of the batter to make more dosas.

13. Ladle the dhal curry into 2 bowls, top with a spoonful of yogurt and serve with the dosas on the side. Garnish with the remaining ¼ cup cilantro.

Sweet Potato and Cabbage Pad Thai

For the Sauce:

2 tablespoons reduced-sodium tamari

2 tablespoons organic crunchy peanut
butter or almond butter

Juice of 1 ½ limes

1 tablespoon sesame oil

1 teaspoon honey

1 teaspoon sriracha

2 tablespoons grated fresh ginger

2 garlic cloves, grated

For the Pad Thai:

¼ cup vegetable oil

1 garlic clove, thinly sliced

2 chilis, thinly sliced

½ cup raw, lightly salted cashews

2 medium sweet potatoes, peeled and
grated

1 small or ½ medium white cabbage, thinly
sliced into "noodles"

2 scallions or spring onions, thinly sliced,
for serving

½ lime, cut into wedges, for serving

1. Make the sauce: Combine the tamari, almond butter, lime juice, sesame oil, honey, and sriracha.

2. Add the grated ginger and garlic to the sauce.

3. Make the pad Thai: Line a plate with paper towels.

4. In a small saucepan over medium heat, heat the oil and add the sliced garlic. Fry until bubbles just stop appearing but before the garlic changes color, about 2 minutes. Use a slotted spoon to transfer to the prepared plate.

5. Add the sliced chilis to this same oil and fry for another minute until the small bubbles stop appearing. Remove with a slotted spoon and reserve the oil.

6. In a large frying pan over medium-high heat, heat 1 table-spoon of the chili-garlic oil and add the sweet potato. Cook until the sweet potato starts to soften, 5 minutes, and add the cabbage and ¼ cup (60 ml) water. Cook until the sweet potato is soft and the cabbage is wilted but hasn't lost its color, 5 minutes.

7. In a small pan over medium heat, add the cashews. Toast for 5 minutes. Remove from the heat and coarsely chop them.

8. Toss the cooked cabbage and sweet potato with the sauce and garnish with the scallions, cashews, fried chili, and fried garlic. Serve with lime wedges on the side.

Socca Bread with Paneer Salad

For the Dressing:

1 tablespoon honey

Juice of ½ lemon

2 tablespoons olive oil

½ teaspoon salt

½ teaspoon cayenne pepper

For the Socca:

½ cup (75 g) chickpea flour

3 tablespoons olive oil

1 teaspoon ground turmeric

1 teaspoon salt

½ teaspoon ground cumin

3 cardamom pods, crushed (see Note)

1 teaspoon coriander seeds

1 red onion, thinly sliced

2 garlic cloves, finely chopped

For the Paneer:

3 ½ ounces (100 g) paneer, cut into 1-centimeter cubes

1 handful of peanuts

¼ teaspoon cayenne pepper

½ teaspoon salt

1 to 2 tablespoons olive oil

For the Salad:

2 handfuls (100 g) of baby spinach

½ red onion

1. Make the dressing: In a small bowl, whisk together the olive oil, honey, lemon juice, salt, and cayenne pepper.

2. Make the socca: Preheat the oven to the Broil/Grill setting at 450°F (230°C).

3. In a medium bowl, add the chickpea flour, ½ cup (120 ml) water, 1 tablespoon of olive oil, the turmeric, salt, and cumin. Mix thoroughly and set aside for 15 minutes.

4. In a cast-iron (or any ovenproof) pan over medium heat, add the crushed cardamom pods, making sure to release the seeds, and the coriander seeds. Toast for 30 seconds before adding the remaining 2 tablespoons olive oil, and the sliced onion. Sweat the onion until it starts to brown, 5 minutes. Add the chopped garlic and cook for 1 to 2 more minutes.

5. Remove the cardamom shells.

6. Pour the batter into the hot pan and transfer the mixture to cook under the hot broiler/grill for 12 minutes.

7. Make the paneer: Line a plate with paper towels and set aside.

8. In a medium bowl, combine the paneer, peanuts, cayenne pepper, and salt.

9. In a nonstick pan over medium-high heat, heat the olive oil. Add the paneer-peanut mixture and fry until both are lightly browned, 2 to 3 minutes.

10. Transfer to the prepared plate.

11. Make the salad: In a medium bowl, toss together the spinach, red onion, peanuts, and paneer. Lightly coat with the dressing.

12. Remove the socca bread from the oven. Let it cool slightly. Slice into quarters and top with the fresh salad.

Note: You can crush cardamom pods in a mortar and pestle or use the back of a knife to gently crack them open, revealing their flavorful seeds.

Tapas Style Tortilla with Confit Peppers

1 pound (450 g) new potatoes, thinly sliced

1 cup plus 1 tablespoon (250 ml) olive oil

1 large or 2 small bell peppers, thinly sliced

2 garlic cloves

A few sprigs of fresh thyme

1 yellow onion, sliced

8 large eggs

Salt and freshly ground black pepper

4 good medium tomatoes or 2 large heritage/heirloom tomatoes, cut into wedges

1 tablespoon balsamic vinegar

Small chunk of Manchego cheese, grated (optional)

1. Preheat the oven to 410°F (210°C).

2. On a baking sheet, toss the sliced potatoes with 1 tablespoon of the olive oil. Bake for 15 to 18 minutes, until beginning to brown and cook through.

3. Switch the oven to the Broil setting at 450°F (230°C).

4. Measure the remaining 1 cup (230 ml) olive oil into a small saucepan and heat over medium-low heat. Add the sliced bell peppers. You don't want it to start smoking or boiling, just a low simmer. Add the thyme and garlic.

5. Cook slowly. If the peppers aren't covered by the oil, use the back of a spoon to press them down gently every 5 minutes until they do. Cook submerged in the oil for 20 to 30 minutes, or until you are ready to serve.

6. Add 1 tablespoon of the olive oil spooned off the top of the bell peppers to a 10-inch nonstick skillet and add the sliced onions. Fry in the oil for 15 minutes until beginning to brown all over. Remove from the heat. Don't clean the pan, just set it aside.

7. Crack the eggs into a bowl, add 1 teaspoon salt, and whisk together. Slowly drizzle 2 tablespoons of the hot oil from the bell peppers into them, continuing to whisk. This will prevent the oil from cooking the eggs.

8. Combine the eggs with the cooked potatoes and caramelized onions in the same bowl.

9. Pour this mixture back into the pan you caramelized the onion with. Place over medium heat. After about 6 minutes, the tortilla should be set around the edge with a slightly runny middle.

10. Transfer the tortilla into the oven and broil for 4 minutes. Remove and allow to cool.

11. In a large bowl, toss the tomatoes with the balsamic vinegar and some salt and pepper. Allow to marinate until ready to serve.

12. Sprinkle the Manchego (if using) over the top of the tomatoes.

13. Drain the peppers and season with salt. Save the olive oil from them for another use!

14. Slice the tortilla into wedges and serve with the bell peppers and the balsamic tomatoes on the side.

Cauliflower Pizza with Sage and Butternut Squash

For the Crust:

1 small to medium head of cauliflower, cut into florets

1 large egg

½ cup (120 g) soft goat cheese

Salt and freshly ground black pepper

For the Toppings:

½ butternut squash, peeled and cut into 1-inch pieces

1 ½ tablespoons olive oil

2 garlic cloves

1 cup (100 g) curly kale, stemmed and chopped

4 ounces (100 g) fresh mozzarella cheese, sliced into ¼-inch-thick rounds

1 large shallot, thinly sliced

About 10 leaves of fresh sage, chopped

About 2 sprigs of fresh rosemary, chopped

1. Make the crust: Preheat the oven to 400°F (200°C). Line a large baking sheet with parchment paper. Set aside.

2. Place the cauliflower florets in a blender and blend until you get a rice-like consistency.

3. Bring a large pot of water to a boil. Add the ground cauliflower to the boiling water. Reduce to a simmer for 1 minute.

4. Drain in a fine mesh sieve, pressing to get the water out, and set aside to cool.

5. In a clean dish towel, squeeze the cauliflower in batches no larger than a tennis ball. Squeeze to drain out as much liquid as possible.

6. The more you squeeze, the better your crust will hold together.

7. In a medium bowl, combine the egg, goat cheese, and a pinch each of salt and pepper.

8. Add the drained cauliflower to the bowl with the egg and goat cheese mixture and combine to form a wet dough.

9. On the prepared baking sheet, spread the dough into a round shape and use your hands to press it about 1/8-inch-thick with a slightly raised rim.

10. Bake for 40 to 45 minutes, until lightly toasted in color. Remove and allow to cool slightly. Keep the oven on.

11. Prepare the toppings: Line a large baking sheet with parchment paper. Set aside.

12. On the prepared baking sheet, toss the squash with 1 tablespoon of olive oil and the garlic and roast for about 30 minutes, until soft. Keep the oven on.

13. Transfer the squash to a large bowl and mash it into a paste using a fork or potato masher. Set aside.

14. Massage the kale with the remaining ½ tablespoon olive oil. Spread the butternut squash over the cauliflower crust.

15. Add the mozzarella, kale, shallot, sage, and rosemary and bake for another 10 minutes, or until the cheese is melted.

Giant Black Bean Burger with Sweet Potato Fries

For the Fries:

2 small sweet potatoes, or 1 large, cut into thin, fry-shaped sticks

2 tablespoons olive oil

1 teaspoon salt

For the Patties:

½ bell pepper, diced

½ small yellow onion, diced

2 garlic cloves, diced

One 14-ounce (400 g) can black beans, drained

2 large eggs

2 tablespoons tomato paste

1 teaspoon ground cumin

1 teaspoon salt

½ teaspoon garlic powder

½ teaspoon smoked paprika

¼ cup (30 g) breadcrumbs

Unsalted butter

2 burger buns

3 tablespoons olive oil

2 slices sharp/mature cheddar cheese

1 head of baby gem lettuce

1 avocado, mashed

1. Make the fries: Preheat the oven to 425°F (215°C). Line a large baking sheet with parchment paper.

2. In a large bowl, toss the sweet potato strips with the olive oil and salt.

3. Lay the sweet potato on a lined baking sheet and bake for 25 to 35 minutes, depending on how thick you've cut them. They should be cooked through and crispy. Keep the oven on and reduce the temperature to 400°F (200°C).

4. Make the patties: Line a large plate with parchment paper. Set aside.

5. In a medium skillet over medium heat, heat 1 tablespoon of the olive oil and add the diced bell pepper, onion, and garlic. Cook until translucent and starting to caramelize, 10 minutes. Allow to cool slightly.

6. In a large bowl, combine the beans, eggs, tomato paste, cumin, garlic powder, salt, and paprika. Mash together with a fork or potato masher to break up the beans. Set aside.

7. Add the bell pepper mixture and the breadcrumbs to the bean mixture. Thoroughly combine.

8. Form the mixture into 2 large balls, squish into patties, and transfer to the prepared plate. Place in the fridge to chill for 10 minutes.

9. Butter the burger buns. Set aside.

10. In an ovenproof griddle pan or flat nonstick pan over medium heat, heat 1 tablespoon of the olive oil. Add the burgers straight from the fridge and cook for about 6 minutes on one side. Drizzle the remaining 1 tablespoon olive oil onto the top before flipping and cooking for another 3 minutes. Add the cheddar and finish in the hot oven for the final 3 to 4 minutes to melt it.

11. Remove the burgers from the pan and place the buns cut-side down on the hot pan to toast briefly.

12. Build your burgers with the lettuce and avocado and serve with the sweet potato fries on the side.

My Favorite French Onion Soup

For the Soup:

3 tablespoons unsalted butter

3 large yellow onions, thinly sliced

2 garlic cloves, sliced

1 teaspoon sugar

4 cups (1 liter) good-quality beef, vegetable, or chicken stock

¼ cup (60 ml) dry white wine

1 dried bay leaf

1 sprig of fresh thyme

1 tablespoon sherry vinegar

Salt and freshly ground black pepper, to taste

For the Croutons:

1 tablespoon unsalted butter

½ baguette (French bread), cut into 4-inch pieces and halved lengthwise

1½ cups (150 g) grated Gruyere cheese

1. Make the soup: In a large, heavy-bottomed pot over medium heat, melt the butter and add the onions. Cook for 10 minutes, until softened. Add the garlic and sugar and increase the heat to medium-high and cook to brown the onions for another 20 minutes.

2. Add the stock, wine, bay leaf, and thyme. Bring to a boil, scraping any browned onions at the bottom of the pot.

3. Reduce the heat, cover, and cook for 30 minutes.

4. Add the sherry vinegar and salt and pepper to taste.

5. Slice the baguette into 4-inch slices and then cut them in half lengthwise and set aside.

6. Make the croutons: Preheat the oven to the Broil/Grill setting at 450°F (230°C).

7. Butter one side of each baguette piece and place them on a baking sheet. Top each with one-quarter of the cheese, pressing to compact it onto the slices.

8. Place the bread under the broiler for 3 to 5 minutes, until the cheese is bubbly and browned and the bread is toasted around the outside.

9. Spoon the soup into 2 bowls and serve each with 2 slices of cheesy bread.

Vegan Mushroom Pho

7 ounces (200 g) shiitake mushrooms or mixed mushrooms

3 scallions or spring onions

2 cups (480 ml) good-quality vegetable stock

3 star anise

3 whole cloves

1 cinnamon stick

1 tablespoon plus 1 teaspoon olive oil

1 large white onion, roughly chopped

2 carrots, roughly chopped

1-inch piece of fresh ginger, thinly sliced

1 teaspoon salt, plus more as needed

4 ½ ounces (130 g) uncooked vermicelli rice noodles

1 tablespoon soy sauce or tamari, plus more to taste

2 heads of bok choy/ baby pak, rinsed thoroughly and thinly sliced

1 handful (15 g) of fresh cilantro/coriander, picked

1 handful (10 g) of fresh mint, picked and roughly chopped

1 to 2 birds-eye chilis (depending on your heat preference), sliced

1 lime, cut into wedges

1. Remove and reserve the stems from the mushrooms. Thinly slice the mushrooms. Set aside.

2. Cut 2 of the scallions into quarters. Thinly slice the remaining scallion. Set aside.

3. In a large saucepan over high heat, add the vegetable stock and 2 cups (280 ml) of water. Add the star anise, cloves, and cinnamon stick and bring to a boil. Reduce to a simmer.

4. In a skillet over high heat, heat 1 teaspoon olive oil along with the onion and carrots. Cook until browned and caramelized, about 10 minutes.

5. Add the onion mixture to the broth.

6. Add the reserved mushroom stems, the scallion quarters, and ginger to the broth. Allow to simmer for 20 minutes.

7. In the same skillet you cooked the onion in over high heat, heat the remaining 1 tablespoon olive oil. Add the sliced mushroom and salt, sautéing until starting to caramelize and tender, about 10 minutes. Remove and allow to cool. Set aside.

8. Place the rice noodles in a large pot. Pour boiling water over the rice noodles to cook until softened, about 8 minutes or according to package instructions. Drain into a colander.

9. Strain the broth through a colander into a large bowl to remove the spices, onion, and mushroom stems. Pour it back into the saucepan. Add the soy sauce. Adjust the seasoning with more soy sauce and salt if needed.

10. Add the bok choy to the broth and bring to a boil before removing from the heat.

11. Place a handful of noodles in the bottom of 2 bowls. Divide the cooked sliced mushrooms, sliced scallions, cilantro, mint, and chilis between the 2 bowls. Ladle the broth over the top. Squeeze lime over everything.

Butternut Squash Vodka Pasta

4 tablespoons olive oil

½ butternut squash, peeled and cut into

1-inch chunks

6 tomatoes, roughly chopped

2 garlic cloves, chopped

1 onion, chopped

2 tablespoons tomato paste

½ cup (100 ml) vodka

½ cup (100 ml) milk (I use almond milk)

2 cups (250 g) penne pasta

Salt and freshly ground black pepper

Grated Parmesan cheese, for serving

1. Pour 1 inch of water into the bottom of a large pan with a steamer basket (or with a metal strainer on top) and set over medium-high heat.

2. Add the butternut squash and steam for 15 minutes, or until soft.

3. Heat 4 tablespoon olive oil in another large pan over medium heat. Add the onion and garlic and cook slowly until caramelized, about 10 minutes.

4. Add the tomato paste and cook for another minute.

5. Add the chopped tomatoes and the vodka and season with salt and pepper. Simmer until the tomatoes are soft.

6. Add the soft butternut squash and the milk to the tomato mixture and cook together for 5 minutes.

7. Bring a pot of salted water to a boil and cook the pasta according to package directions.

8. Combine the tomato and onion mixture with the butternut squash by placing it in a blender and blending until completely smooth. Pour over the pasta, mixing to combine.

9. Top with grated Parmesan and black pepper.

Sweet Potato Gnocchi with Red Pesto

For the Pesto:

½ cup (30 g) oil-packed sun-dried tomatoes

1/3 cup (70 g) extra-virgin olive oil (or use the sun-dried tomato oil instead for added flavor)

¼ cup (35 g) raw, unsalted cashews

¼ cup (25 g) grated Parmesan cheese

1 garlic clove

Juice of ½ lemon

⅛ teaspoon chili flakes (optional)

¼ teaspoon salt

Freshly ground black pepper

For the Gnocchi:

1 medium sweet potato

½ cup (125 g) ricotta cheese

¼ cup (25 g) grated Parmesan cheese

Salt

2/3 cup (85 g) all-purpose flour (gluten-free if needed), plus more for dusting

1 tablespoon olive oil

1. Make the pesto: In a blender or the bowl of a food processor, add the sun-dried tomatoes, olive oil, cashews, Parmesan, garlic, lemon juice, chili flakes (if using), salt, and pepper. Process until well incorporated. Set aside.

2. Make the gnocchi: Preheat the oven to 425°F (215°C). Line a baking sheet with foil.

3. Use a fork to prick holes into the sweet potato. Place on the baking sheet and bake for about 45 minutes, until soft. Remove from the oven and let cool.

4. Scoop out the sweet potato flesh.

5. In a large bowl, combine the ricotta, half of the Parmesan, and a pinch of salt. Add the sweet potato flesh. Combine until smooth.

6. Measure 2/3 cup of the flour and sift it into a separate bowl.

7. Add the flour to the ricotta mixture and mix well with a spoon. Don't overmix; this ensures the dough remains slightly fluffy in texture.

8. Lightly dust your work surface with flour.

9. Take a portion of the dough, similar in size to a tennis ball, and roll the dough with both hands into a long snake shape.

10. Cut into 1-inch pieces. Repeat until all the dough is used.

11. Bring a large pot of salted water to a boil. Add the gnocchi, working in batches so as not to overcrowd the pot. Allow to float to the surface before removing with a slotted spoon.

12. In a large skillet over high heat, heat the olive oil and pan-fry the finished gnocchi and add the pesto to coat. Top with the remaining 2 tablespoons Parmesan cheese.

LA's Best Fried Tofu Bowl

1 cup (200 g) uncooked brown rice

1 medium bunch of curly kale, stemmed and roughly chopped

½ cup (50 g) unsweetened coconut flakes

1/3 cup (20 g) nutritional yeast

¼ teaspoon salt

2 tablespoons olive oil

For the Dressing:

1 lime

¼ cup (60 ml) olive oil

1 ½ tablespoons tahini

1 tablespoon soy sauce

1 tablespoon honey

1 teaspoon toasted sesame oil

For the Tofu:

One 16-ounce block firm or extra-firm tofu

2 tablespoons corn starch

½ teaspoon salt

½ teaspoon freshly ground black pepper

2 tablespoons vegetable oil

1. Preheat the oven to 375°F (190°C). Line a large baking sheet with parchment paper. Set aside.

2. In a small pot with a lid, add the rice and 2 cups (475 ml) of water. Bring the rice and water to a boil, then reduce the heat to a simmer, cover, and allow to cook until all the water is absorbed, about 20 minutes. Leaving the lid on, remove the pot from the heat and allow it to steam for another 10 minutes.

3. In a large bowl, toss the kale, coconut, nutritional yeast, salt, and olive oil. Place on the prepared baking sheet and roast, tossing halfway through, until the kale is crispy and the coconut is golden, about 10 minutes. Keep an eye on this to make sure your kale doesn't burn.

4. Make the dressing: Finely grate the zest of the lime directly into a bowl; halve the lime and squeeze in the juice.

5. Add the olive oil, tahini, soy sauce, honey, and sesame oil. Set aside.

6. Prepare the tofu: Remove the tofu from its packaging and place it on a plate. Use paper towels or a clean kitchen towel to gently press out the excess liquid from the tofu block.

7. Cut the tofu into 1-inch cubes.

8. In a large bowl, combine the corn starch with the salt and pepper and mix well. Add the tofu cubes to the bowl and toss to coat evenly.

9. Line a plate with paper towels. Set aside.

10. In a nonstick skillet or cast-iron pan over medium-high heat, heat the vegetable oil. Add the coated tofu cubes, spread them out in the pan, and let them cook without moving them for 3 to 4 minutes. Flip the tofu cubes and cook until golden brown and crispy on all sides, another 3 to 4 minutes.

11. Remove the tofu from the pan and drain onto the prepared plate.

12. In a large bowl, toss the rice with the crispy kale, coconut, and tofu. Pour in the dressing and toss until everything is combined.

13. Split between 2 bowls and serve with lime wedges.

Kimchee Fried Forbidden Rice Bowl

For the Sauce:

2 tablespoons soy sauce

1 tablespoon gochujang sauce, plus more for serving (you can also use chili garlic sauce here)

1 tablespoon toasted sesame oil

½-inch piece of fresh ginger

For the Rice:

1 cup (200 g) uncooked black/forbidden or jasmine rice

2 tablespoons olive oil

1 small onion, finely chopped

2 garlic cloves, finely chopped

2 cups (150 g) shiitake mushrooms, stemmed and sliced

2 bunches of baby bok choy/pak choi, rinsed thoroughly, trimmed, and thinly sliced

1 cup (150 g) kimchee, roughly chopped

Salt and freshly ground black pepper, to taste

For the Eggs:

1 tablespoon toasted sesame oil

1 teaspoon gochujang sauce (you can use chili garlic sauce here if you can't find gochujang)

2 large eggs

Salt

For Serving:

1 sheet nori (seaweed), cut into thin strips

2 scallions or spring onions, thinly sliced

1 tablespoon sesame seeds

1. Make the sauce: In a small bowl, whisk together the soy sauce, gochujang, and sesame oil. Grate in the ginger and combine. Set aside.

2. Make the rice: In a medium pot with a lid, combine the rice with 2 cups (470 ml) water. Bring to a boil, place the lid on the pot, and cook until the water has all been absorbed. The cook time will depend on the type of rice used, so check the package for instructions. Remove from the heat. Leave covered for another 10 minutes.

3. In a large skillet over medium heat, heat the olive oil. Add the onion and garlic. Cook until the onion is translucent, about 5 minutes.

4. Add the mushrooms and increase the heat so they are crisping up slightly in the pan. Make sure the onions and garlic are not burning.

5. Once these are crisped but tender on the inside, 5 to 7 minutes more, add the sliced bok choy and kimchee and cook until the bok choy has wilted slightly, another 2 minutes. Scrape any browned bits off the bottom of the pan using the liquid from the kimchee and bok choy.

6. Add the cooked rice and the sauce and increase the heat slightly to fry it all together for 5 minutes. Add salt and pepper to taste. Remove from the heat.

7. Make the eggs: In a nonstick or cast-iron skillet over medium-high heat, heat the sesame oil and gochujang until both are sizzling. Gently mix with the back of a spoon so the gochujang is evenly distributed.

8. Crack the eggs into the sauce and cook until the whites are set but the yolks are still runny, 2 to 3 minutes. Season with salt.

9. Spoon the fried rice into 2 bowls. Top with the fried eggs. Sprinkle the scallions, sesame seeds, and nori strips over the top.

James' Butternut Squash Curry

1 cup brown rice

1 large shallot, halved

2 garlic cloves

1 to 2 red chilis (depending on heat preference)

1-inch piece of fresh ginger

Salt

1 tablespoon olive oil

2 teaspoons ground turmeric

1 teaspoon ground cumin

1 teaspoon ground coriander

One 14-ounce (400 ml) can full-fat coconut milk

One 14-ounce (400 ml) can chopped tomatoes

2 large, sweet potatoes, peeled and roughly chopped

1 small or ½ large butternut squash, peeled and roughly chopped

2 large handfuls of baby spinach

¼ bunch of fresh cilantro/coriander, roughly chopped, for serving

Lime wedges, for serving

½ cup Greek yogurt, for serving

1. In a medium pot with a lid, combine the rice with 2 cups (470 ml) water. Bring to a boil, cover with a lid, and allow to simmer for 20 minutes, or until cooked through. Remove from the heat. Leave the lid on to steam the rice.

2. In a blender or the bowl of a food processor, add the shallot, garlic, chilis, ginger, a large pinch of salt, and ½ cup (100 ml) water. Blend to a fine paste. Add more salt to taste.

3. In a large pot over medium heat, heat the olive oil. Add the shallot paste and cook until the liquid has mostly evaporated and the paste is sputtering, 5 to 8 minutes.

4. Add the turmeric, cumin, and ground coriander. Cook until fragrant, 30 seconds.

5. Add the coconut milk and chopped tomatoes. Fill one of the empty cans with water and add that as well. Bring to a boil, then reduce to a simmer.

6. Add the chopped sweet potatoes and squash. If there is not enough liquid to cover the vegetables, add some water until they are submerged. Cover and cook for 30 minutes.

7. If you want to mash the squash and potato, use a fork or potato masher to gently mash the curry.

8. Fold in the baby spinach.

9. Serve hot over the rice. Serve with the chopped cilantro and lime wedges. Top with a dollop of yogurt.

Fresh Salmon Poke Bowl

1 cup (200 g) uncooked brown rice, rinsed

2 tablespoons rice vinegar

1 tablespoon sugar

½ cucumber, thinly sliced

¼ small purple cabbage, thinly sliced

Salt

5 tablespoons tamari or soy sauce

1 ½ tablespoons toasted sesame oil

Pinkie finger-size piece of fresh ginger

4 scallions or spring onions, thinly sliced

2/3 pound (300 g) sushi-grade salmon (or tuna), skin removed and cubed

6 radishes, thinly sliced

1 carrot, thinly sliced

1 avocado, pitted and sliced

1 chili (optional), thinly sliced, for serving

1 mango, cubed, for serving

1. In a medium pot with a lid, combine the rice with 2 cups (470 ml) water. Bring to a boil, reduce to a simmer, and cover with a lid for 10 minutes, or until the rice is cooked and the water is absorbed. Remove from the heat. Leave the lid on to steam the rice.

2. In a small pan, combine the rice wine vinegar, ½ cup (110 ml) water, and the sugar. Bring to a boil and remove from the heat.

3. Add the sliced cucumber to the pan and set aside for at least 15 minutes to pickle.

4. Massage the sliced cabbage slightly with a pinch of salt. Place it in a colander over the sink to allow the excess liquid to run off.

5. In a large bowl, whisk together the soy sauce and sesame oil. Grate the ginger into the sauce and add the scallions.

7. Toss the salmon in the soy-sesame sauce and place in the fridge until you are ready to serve.

8. Pour the excess liquid off the cabbage and pickled cucumbers.

9. If cooking the salmon, pour the contents of the sauce and salmon into a small pot and cook slowly over low heat, stirring gently once, until the salmon turns opaque, 5 to 10 minutes. Otherwise, serve raw.

10. Assemble the bowls: Top the rice with the salmon (pour extra sauce over the rice), the pickled cucumber, cabbage, radishes, carrot, and avocado. Top with the mango and chili (if using).

Grilled Peri-Peri Prawns with Sweet Corn, Avocado, and Feta

For the Peri-Peri Sauce:

1 red bell pepper, seeded and quartered

3 red bird's eye chilis, stemmed

8 unpeeled garlic cloves

½ cup (120 ml) extra-virgin olive oil

3 tablespoons red or white wine vinegar

2 teaspoons salt

½ teaspoon smoked paprika

For the Prawns:

1 pound (450 g) raw jumbo prawns (these can be fresh or frozen), peeled and deveined

1 tablespoon olive oil

2 cups (328 g) frozen corn, thawed (see Note)

1 ripe avocado, pitted and cubed

7 ounces (200 g) feta cheese, cubed

1 tablespoon unsalted butter

2 large slices sourdough toast

Juice of 1 lime, for serving

1. Make the peri-peri sauce: Preheat the oven to the Broil/Grill setting at 450°F (230°C). Place an oven rack in the top third of the oven.

2. Place the bell pepper, chilis, and garlic on an oven tray and place under the broiler/grill. Cook until starting to char, 5 minutes. Remove and flip to cook the other side under the broiler. Continue to grill/broil until charred all over, another 5 minutes. Remove and allow to cool.

3. Peel the garlic once it's cooled slightly.

4. In a blender or the bowl of a food processor, add the bell pepper, chilis, garlic, olive oil, red wine vinegar, salt, and paprika. Blend well. Transfer half of the sauce to a large bowl and reserve the rest. Set aside.

5. Prepare the prawns: If your prawns are frozen, run them under room-temperature water for a few minutes until defrosted.

6. Add the cleaned prawns to the bowl with half of the sauce, tossing to coat. Set aside.

7. In a large skillet over high heat, heat the olive oil and add the corn with a pinch of salt. Continue to cook, stirring until the corn is starting to char and pop (this should happen quickly). Remove from the pan, allow to cool, and add to a large bowl.

8. Add the feta and avocado to the bowl with the corn.

9. In the same skillet you used for the corn over high heat, add the coated prawns. Cook until curling up and opaque, 1 to 2 minutes per side.

10. Stir the prawns into the corn, avocado, and feta mixture.

11. Butter the bread and add it to the same pan over medium-high heat, butter-side down, until you have a nice, toasted side. Remove and place on 2 plates, toasted-side up.

12. Top with the prawn salad. Drizzle more sauce over it if you like things very spicy. Squeeze the lime juice over the top.

Note: To thaw the frozen corn quickly, you can rinse it under warm water.

Baja-Style Fish Tacos with Fresh Corn Tortillas

For the Slaw:

1 handful of cilantro/coriander

¼ cup (70 g) plain Greek yogurt

Zest and juice of 1/2 lime

Salt

1/2 small red cabbage, thinly sliced

For the Salsa:

3 to 4 medium tomatoes

1/2 onion

1 red chili

1 unpeeled garlic clove

Juice of 1 lime

1 teaspoon cumin seeds

½ teaspoon honey

½ teaspoon salt

For the Fish:

½ cup (50 g) almond flour

1 teaspoon paprika

½ teaspoon garlic powder

Salt

1/3 cup (45 g) gluten-free or all-purpose flour

1 large egg

Olive oil

12 ounces (340 g) cod, cut into 1 ½-inch strips and pat dry

Fresh Tortillas, for serving (recipe follows), or 8 store-bought tortillas

1. Make the slaw: Pick the leaves off the cilantro and reserve the remaining stems for the salsa. Set aside.

2. In a medium bowl, combine the yogurt with the lime zest and juice. Season with salt to taste. Add the cabbage and cilantro leaves and toss.

3. Make the salsa: Preheat the oven to the Broil/Grill setting at the highest heat. Line a large baking sheet with parchment paper.

4. Cut the onion half in half.

5. Place the tomatoes, onion quarters, chili, and garlic on the prepared baking sheet and cook under the broiler/grill until blistered, tossing halfway through, 5 to 10 minutes. Allow to cool.

6. Peel the tomatoes and garlic. Discard the skins.

7. In a blender or food processor, add the tomatoes, onions, chili garlic, lime juice, cumin seeds, honey, salt, and the reserved cilantro stems. Blend to your desired consistency. Set aside.

8. Make the fish: Prepare 3 bowls to bread the fish: In a large, shallow bowl, whisk together the almond flour, paprika, garlic powder, and a large pinch of salt. In a separate shallow bowl, add the gluten-free flour. In a third shallow bowl, add and whisk the egg.

9. Preheat a frying pan over medium-high heat, covering the base of the pan about ½ inch (1 centimeter) of olive oil.

10. Dip the fish first in the gluten-free flour, shaking to remove excess, then in the egg, then in the almond flour mixture.

11. Working in batches, pan-fry the fish until golden, about 2 minutes per side. Repeat with all the strips.

12. Build the tacos by placing the fish on the tortillas and topping with the slaw and salsa.

Tortilla Recipe

TORTILLAS

Makes 8 to 10 tortillas

1 ½ cups (90 g) masa harina

1 cup (120 ml) water

1. In a large bowl, stir together the masa harina and water.

2. Knead together until you have a smooth, even texture.

3. Set up the tortilla press by putting plastic wrap over both sides.

4. Form small balls and press them between both sides of the tortilla press to form a flat tortilla.

5. Set up 2 skillets, preferably nonstick or cast-iron, on the stove. One should be over medium heat and the other over high heat.

6. Cook the pressed tortilla in the high-heat pan for 30 seconds. Use a spatula to flip it onto the second, medium-heat pan and cook the other side for another 30 seconds. Flip again onto the first side in the same medium-heat pan. Remove from the heat after a final 30 seconds.

7. Repeat with the rest of the dough.

Tuna Tataki Nicoise Salad

For the Rub:

1 tablespoon nigella (black onion) seeds

1 tablespoon white sesame seeds

½ teaspoon salt

For the Dressing:

¼ cup (50 g) pitted olives (I like Castel-vetrano, but black Niçoise are the classic)

2 ½ tablespoons olive oil

1 tablespoon red wine vinegar

Juice of ½ lemon

1 garlic clove

Salt and freshly ground black pepper

For the Salad:

3 large eggs

6 ounces (300 g) tuna steak

1 small head of broccoli, cut into florets

7 ounces (200 g) green beans, ends trimmed

1 head baby gem lettuce, torn and cut into small pieces

7 ounces (200 g) halved cherry tomatoes

1 tablespoon olive oil

Sesame and nigella seeds, for serving

1. Make the rub: In a small bowl, combine the nigella seeds, sesame seeds, and salt. Set aside.

2. Make the dressing: In a blender or bowl of a food processor, add the olives, olive oil, vinegar, lemon juice, and garlic. Add salt and pepper to taste. Set aside.

3. Make the salad: Bring a medium pot of water to a boil. Fill two bowls with ice and cold water. Set aside.

4. Use a spoon to slowly lower the eggs into it without breaking. Remove the eggs after 6 ½ minutes and allow to cool in one of the ice baths.

5. Bring a second, larger pot to boil. Add the broccoli and cook until a butter knife slides through, 3 to 5 minutes. Transfer to the second ice bath. Keep the boiling water.

6. Add the green beans to the boiling water for 1 minute. Transfer to the ice water with the broccoli and drain both into a colander.

7. Cut the tuna into rectangular blocks that are about 2 to 3 inches in length. The more rectangular the pieces, the easier it will be to cook. Pat the fish dry.

8. Gently add the rub over the tuna, creating a crust.

9. In a skillet over medium heat, heat the olive oil. Add the tuna slices and cook one side for 30 seconds. Flip onto the side to cook for another 30 seconds. Continue this until all 4 edges are equally cooked. The middle should still be raw. Place the fish on a plate and into the fridge to stop the cooking.

10. Remove the cooled eggs from the ice water. Carefully peel them and cut in half.

11. Remove the tuna from the fridge and slice thinly to reveal the pink center.

12. Toss the lettuce, the broccoli, green beans, and cherry tomatoes with the dressing.

13. Divide between 2 plates and top with the sliced tuna, eggs, and sesame and nigella seeds.

Vietnamese-Style Shrimp & Rice Noodle Salad

For the Shrimp:

½ pound (250 g) fresh or frozen raw shrimp/

prawns (I like jumbo), peeled and deveined

½ bunch of fresh mint

½ bunch of fresh cilantro/coriander

1 large shallot

3 garlic cloves

1 red chili (optional)

Juice of 1 lime

2 tablespoons brown sugar

1 tablespoon olive oil

1 tablespoon fish sauce

½ tablespoon soy sauce (gluten-free if needed)

For the Salad:

7 ounces (200 g) uncooked rice vermicelli

noodles

1 large carrot, grated

1 red bell pepper, cut into matchsticks

1 small cucumber, cut into matchsticks

1 head baby gem lettuce, sliced into thin

ribbons

For the Nuoc Cham Dressing:

2 garlic cloves, finely chopped

1 chili, finely chopped

¼ cup (120 ml) fish sauce

Juice of 1 lime

2 tablespoons rice vinegar

1 tablespoon brown sugar

½ cup (120 ml) cold water

1 red chili, sliced, for serving

Fresh mint sprigs, for serving

1. Prepare the shrimp: If your shrimp are frozen, run them under room-temperature water for a few minutes until defrosted.

2. Separate the leaves from the stems of the mint and cilantro Reserve the mint and cilantro leaves for the salad and set aside. Reserve the mint and cilantro stems.

3. In a blender or the bowl of a food processor, add the mint and cilantro stems along with the shallot, garlic, chili (if using), lime juice, brown sugar, olive oil, fish sauce, and soy sauce.

4. Pour into a medium bowl and add the prawns. Place the bowl in the refrigerator to marinate for at least 10 minutes while you make the salad.

5. Make the salad: Boil water in a kettle.

6. In a large bowl, add the vermicelli noodles and soak in the boiling water for 5 minutes, or until they are tender. Drain into a colander and rinse with cold water until the noodles are room temperature. Return to the bowl.

7. Add the carrot, bell pepper, cucumber, lettuce, and reserved mint and cilantro leaves to the bowl with the cooked rice noodles.

8. Make the dressing: In a small bowl, whisk together the garlic, chili, fish sauce, lime juice, rice vinegar, brown sugar, and cold water.

9. Assemble the bowls: Remove the shrimp from the fridge and drain the excess marinade.

10. In a frying pan over high heat, heat the olive oil. Add the shrimp. Flip after 1 minute. They should cook through quickly, get a crispy exterior, and turn from clear to opaque (white). Toss the shrimp once more to ensure they cook evenly and remove from the heat. They should take about 3 minutes total.

11. Toss the salad with the dressing.

12. Top with the cooked prawns, sliced chili, and mint sprigs, and enjoy at room temperature.

Pomegranate Salmon with Jewelled Rice

For the Salmon:

2 tablespoons pomegranate molasses

1 tablespoon olive oil

Juice of ½ lime

½ teaspoon salt

Two 4-ounce salmon filets (225 g)

For the Rice:

2 tablespoons (30 g) unsalted butter

1 carrot, shredded

1 onion, thinly sliced

½ cup (70 g) pine nuts

1 cinnamon stick

3 whole cloves

3 cardamom pods

1 star anise

1 cup (180 g) uncooked basmati rice

1/3 cup (50 g) raisins

¼ cup (50 g) apricots, chopped

½ cup (87 g) fresh pomegranate seeds, for serving

1. Make the salmon: Preheat the oven to 400°F (200°C). Line a baking sheet with parchment paper. Set aside.

2. In a large bowl, whisk together the pomegranate molasses, olive oil, lime juice, and salt.

3. Add the salmon filets and toss in the molasses marinade. Cover and refrigerate for about 20 minutes.

4. Make the rice: In a large skillet or pot with a lid over medium-high heat, melt the butter. Add the onion and carrot and cook until browning, about 10 minutes. Remove from the pan.

5. In the same skillet over medium-high heat, add the pine nuts, cinnamon stick, cloves, cardamom, and star anise and toast for 2 minutes.

6. Add the rice and cook for another minute with the spices. Return the cooked onion and carrot to the skillet. Stir to combine.

7. Add the raisins and chopped apricots.

8. Pour 1 ¼ cups (300 ml) water over the top and fit with a lid. Cook on very low heat for 12 minutes. Remove from the heat and let sit, covered, for another 10 minutes.

9. Remove the salmon from the fridge and let it come to room temperature.

10. Place on the prepared baking sheet. Reserve the marinade left in the bowl and set aside. Bake the salmon for 10 minutes, or until cooked through.

11. Pour the remaining pomegranate marinade into a small saucepan and bring to a boil. Reduce to a simmer for 5 minutes, or until you have a nice shiny glaze.

12. Uncover the rice and scoop it onto 2 plates. Top with the salmon, spooning the glaze over the top, and sprinkle over with the pomegranate seeds.

Thai-Style Fish Cakes and Papaya Salad

For the Fish Cakes:

10 extra fine green beans, roughly sliced

1 shoot lemongrass, roughly sliced

3 scallions or spring onions, roughly sliced

1 ½ tablespoons fish sauce

1 tablespoon Thai red curry paste

1 small handful of cilantro/coriander, plus more for serving

1 tablespoon sugar

1 tablespoon fresh lime juice

1 large egg

Two 8-ounce filets white fish (cod, haddock, whiting, or sole), skin removed and diced (500 g)

2 tablespoons breadcrumbs

1 teaspoon salt

2 tablespoons peanuts

3 tablespoons olive oil

For the Salad:

2 handfuls (100 g) of extra fine green beans, ends trimmed

1 to 2 red bird's eye chilis (depending on your heat preference), stemmed, plus more thinly sliced for serving

1 small garlic clove, halved

2 tablespoons sugar

4 cherry tomatoes

1 ½ tablespoons fish sauce

2 tablespoons fresh lime juice

1 carrot, shredded

1 small or 1/2 medium papaya, seeded and cubed

1. Make the fish cakes: Preheat the oven to 330°F (165°C).

2. In a blender or the bowl of a food processor, add the green beans, lemongrass, scallions, fish sauce, curry paste, cilantro, sugar, 2 tablespoons water, 1 tablespoon of the lime juice, and the egg. Blend.

3. Add the diced fish, breadcrumbs, and salt. Blitz to a smooth paste.

4. Scoop this paste into 8 even balls and press down into burger-shaped patties. Place these in the fridge to chill for 5 minutes.

5. In a large ovenproof skillet over medium-high heat, add the peanuts and toast until starting to brown and giving off a nutty odour, 1 to 2 minutes. Remove and set aside.

6. Add the olive oil to the pan and add the fish cakes. Fry for 5 minutes on each side, then transfer to the oven to cook for 5 more minutes.

7. Make the salad: In a mortar and pestle, add the green beans, chilis, garlic, and sugar. Pound to combine. If you don't have a mortar and pestle, you can place the ingredients in a medium bowl and use the edge of a heavy glass to crush them.

8. Add the tomatoes and crush for a final time.

9. Add the fish sauce and lime juice. Add the papaya and carrot and allow to marinate together for 5 minutes.

10. Divide the salad between 2 plates and serve with the fish cakes on top. Garnish with the toasted peanuts, cilantro, and sliced chilis.

The Healthiest Chicken Caesar Salad

For the Dressing:

2 anchovy filets

1 garlic clove

Juice of ½ lemon

2 tablespoons olive oil

2 teaspoons soy sauce

2 tablespoons (11 g) grated Parmesan cheese

1/3 cup (85 g) plain Greek yogurt

Salt and freshly ground black pepper, to taste

For the Chicken Salad:

1 large bunch of curly or lacinato/Cavolo Nero kale, stemmed and torn into bite-size pieces

1 tablespoon plus 1 teaspoon olive oil

¾ teaspoon salt

Two 6-ounce chicken breasts (340 g)

1 teaspoon paprika

½ cup (70 g) unsalted, raw cashews

2 ripe avocados, pitted and cut into bite-size pieces

Freshly ground black pepper, for serving

2 tablespoons (11 g) grated Parmesan cheese, for serving

1. Make the dressing: In a medium bowl, mash the anchovy filets against the side of the bowl with a fork, breaking them down.

2. Grate the garlic into the same bowl. Add the lemon juice, olive oil, soy sauce, grated cheese, and Greek yogurt. Mix well to combine. Add salt and black pepper to taste. Set aside.

3. Make the chicken salad: Preheat the oven to 400°F (200°C).

4. Rinse and dry the kale well. In a large bowl, add the kale, 1 teaspoon of the olive oil, and ¼ teaspoon of the salt. Massage the kale for 2 minutes. Set aside.

5. Pat the chicken breasts dry with paper towels and season by rubbing the paprika and the remaining ½ teaspoon salt evenly over them.

6. In an ovenproof frying pan over high heat, heat the remaining 1 tablespoon olive oil until it sizzles. Add the chicken breasts. Cook until browned, 1 to 2 minutes per side, then transfer to the oven to cook the chicken for another 10 minutes. Remove from the oven and allow the chicken to rest in the pan for another 10 minutes.

7. Thinly slice the chicken against the grain.

8. In a small pan over medium heat, add the cashews and toast until browned and giving off a nice, nutty smell, 3 to 5 minutes. Transfer to a cutting board and crush with the back of a spoon.

9. Divide the avocados, kale, cashews, and half of the dressing between 2 medium bowls.

10. Toss to combine everything and taste. Add more dressing to your preference.

11. Top the salads with the chicken. Serve with more grated cheese and more black pepper.

Crispy Coconut and Almond Chicken with Roasted Tomato & Arugula Salad

For the Roasted Tomatoes:

6 ounces (170 g) cherry tomatoes

¼ tablespoon olive oil

For the Chicken:

Two 6-ounce chicken breasts (340 g)

½ cup (60 g) almond flour

½ cup (45 g) shredded, unsweetened coconut

1 teaspoon paprika

¼ teaspoon salt

¼ teaspoon freshly ground black pepper

¾ cup (90 g) all-purpose or gluten-free flour

1 large egg

Splash of milk of choice

2 tablespoons unsalted butter

2 tablespoons vegetable oil

For the Arugula Salad:

4 cups (100 g) arugula/rocket

1 small handful of fresh cilantro/coriander leaves, roughly chopped

Parmesan cheese shavings (optional)

Pinch of salt

1. Make the roasted tomatoes: Preheat the oven to 400°F (200°C).

2. On a small baking sheet, toss the cherry tomatoes with the olive oil, and bake for 10 minutes. Remove from the oven and set aside.

3. Make the chicken: Place the chicken breasts between 2 pieces of parchment paper and using a meat mallet, rolling pin, or wine or water bottle, gently pound them out to ¾-inch (2-centimeter) thickness.

4. Prepare 2 plates for breading the chicken: On one, whisk together the almond flour, coconut, paprika, 1/8 teaspoon of salt, and the pepper.

5. On the second plate, whisk together the flour and the remaining 1/8 teaspoon salt.

6. In a shallow bowl, whisk egg with your milk of choice.

7. Dip the flattened chicken first into the flour, shaking to remove excess flour, then into the egg, then finally into the almond and coconut mixture, coating evenly.

8. In a large skillet or cast-iron pan over medium-high heat, melt the butter and vegetable oil.

9. Place one chicken breast in the pan and cook for 5 minutes on each side. Repeat with the second flattened chicken.

10. Make the salad: Toss the roasted tomatoes with the arugula, cilantro, shaved Parmesan, and salt.

11. Serve the chicken with the salad and roasted tomatoes.

Korean-Style Pork Noodles and Pickled Cucumber

For the Pickled Cucumbers:

1 tablespoon rice vinegar

1 teaspoon sugar

½ teaspoon salt

½ large or 1 small cucumber, seeded and sliced

1 teaspoon sesame seeds

For the Noodles:

2 tablespoons gochujang (or chili garlic paste)

1 tablespoon soy sauce

1 tablespoon sugar

1 finger-size piece of fresh ginger

3 ½ ounces (100 g) uncooked rice noodles

2 tablespoons olive oil

1 large onion, finely diced

1 red bell pepper, finely diced

2 garlic cloves, finely diced

½ pound (250 g) ground pork

1 bunch of spring greens, collard greens, Chinese cabbage, or kale, thinly sliced

2 scallions or spring onions, thinly sliced, for serving

1. Make the pickled cucumbers: In a medium bowl, whisk together the rice vinegar, sugar, and salt.

2. Toss the sliced cucumber in the rice vinegar mixture with the sesame seeds. Set aside to marinate.

3. Make the noodles: In a small bowl, whisk together the gochujang, soy sauce, sugar, and 1 cup (240 ml) water. Grate the ginger into it. Set aside.

4. Cook the rice noodles according to the package instructions, then run under cold water to stop the cooking.

5. In a large skillet over medium-high heat, heat 1 tablespoon of the olive oil and add the onion, bell pepper, and garlic. Cook until starting to brown and soften, about 10 minutes.

6. Remove the cooked vegetables from the pan. Add the remaining 1 tablespoon olive oil and the pork, breaking the meat up until it's brown and cooked through, 7 minutes.

7. Return the vegetables to the pan, along with the sliced greens.

8. Add the gochujang sauce. Bring to a boil.

9. Add the cooked noodles, tossing to combine.

10. Spoon the noodle mixture into bowls and top with the pickled cucumber and scallions.

Lamb and Pistachio Kofta Salad

For the Koftas:

1 shallot

¼ cup (30 g) shelled pistachios

4 sprigs of mint, including stems

Zest of 1 lemon

1 tablespoon ground cumin

½ tablespoon chilli powder

1 teaspoon salt

½ pound (250 g) lamb mince

2 teaspoons olive oil

2 pita breads

For the Tzatziki:

¼ large cucumber

1 medium garlic clove

¾ cup (175 g) plain Greek yogurt

Juice of ½ lemon

½ teaspoon fine sea salt

For the Salad:

2 medium heirloom tomatoes, sliced

¾ large cucumber, halved lengthwise
and sliced into half moons

1 small red onion, thinly sliced

2 teaspoons olive oil

1 teaspoon sherry vinegar

3 ½ ounces (100 g) feta cheese

Freshly ground black pepper

1. Make the koftas: Preheat the oven to the Broil/Grill setting at 450°F (230°C).

2. In a blender or the bowl of a food processor, add the shallot, pistachios, mint, lemon zest, cumin, chili powder, and salt. Blitz until the ingredients are fine and blended. Add the lamb and pulse for another 30 seconds until just combined.

3. Form the meat into 6 equal portions and roll each one into a cylindrical or oval shape, ensuring that they are evenly formed. Lightly drizzle the oil over the kebabs and use your hands to roll them in it, ensuring an even coating.

4. Place the koftas on a grill-safe tray under the broiler/grill, turning every few minutes until all sides are evenly cooked to golden brown. Remove and allow to cool.

5. Turn off the broiler/grill and toss the pita breads into the hot oven for 1 minute to warm slightly.

6. Make the tzatziki: In a medium bowl, add the Greek yogurt, lemon juice, and salt. Grate in the cucumber and garlic. Stir to combine.

7. Make the salad: Arrange the sliced tomatoes on a plate.

8. In a bowl, toss together the cucumber, onion, olive oil, and vinegar. Season with salt and pepper.

9. Spread the cucumber and onion mixture on top of the sliced tomatoes and crumble the feta over the top. Crack the black pepper over the salad.

10. Top the salad with the kofta and tzatziki and serve with the warm pita on the side.

Mediterranean Quinoa with Blackened Chicken

For the Chicken and Quinoa:

2 teaspoons salt

1 ½ teaspoons garlic powder

1 teaspoon ground white pepper

1 teaspoon onion powder

1 teaspoon chili powder

1 teaspoon dried oregano

1 teaspoon dried thyme

1 teaspoon smoked paprika

Two 6-ounce boneless, skinless chicken breasts (340 g)

5 tablespoons olive oil

½ cup (70 g) pumpkin seeds

½ cup uncooked quinoa

For the Salad:

1 cup arugula/rocket

½ cucumber, diced

¾ cup (110 g) cherry tomatoes, quartered

½ cup (100 g) feta cheese, diced

1 shallot, finely chopped

1 handful of fresh basil

½ cup raw, unsalted cashews

Juice of 1 lemon

1 tablespoon honey

1 garlic clove

½ teaspoon salt

1. Preheat the oven to 400°F (200°C).

2. In a large shallow bowl, whisk together the salt, garlic powder, white pepper, onion powder, chili powder, oregano, thyme, and paprika.

3. Dredge the chicken in the spice mix so they are thoroughly coated.

4. In an ovenproof frying pan or cast-iron skillet over medium heat, heat ½ tablespoon of the olive oil. Add the pumpkin seeds, toasting until they start to brown and make a popping noise, about 2 minutes. Remove them from the pan.

5. Add 2 more tablespoons of olive oil to the pan and increase the heat slightly. Add the chicken breasts and cook until the spice mixture is turning black and forming a crust around the chicken, 2 minutes per side. Transfer the pan to the oven and bake for 8 minutes. Remove the chicken from the oven, place on a cutting board, and allow to rest for 10 minutes.

6. In a fine-mesh sieve, rinse the quinoa under running water briefly.

7. In a large skillet or shallow pot with a lid, add the quinoa and 1 cup (230 ml) water. Bring to a boil. Reduce to a simmer and cook, covered, until the liquid has been absorbed and the quinoa is tender, another 10 to 15 minutes. Remove from the heat and allow to rest, covered.

8. Make the salad: Add the cashews to a small bowl and cover with boiling water. Let soak for 15 minutes, until softened. Drain.

9. Separate the leaves from the stems of the basil. Reserve the stems. Chop the leaves.

10. In a large bowl, add half of the chopped basil, the arugula, cucumber, cherry tomatoes, feta, and shallot.

11. In a blender or the bowl of a food processor, add the soaked cashews, ½ cup water, the basil stems, the remaining half of the basil leaves, the lemon juice, honey, garlic, and salt. Blend to form a dressing.

12. Add the quinoa to the salad and toss. Add the toasted pumpkin seeds.

13. Slice the rested blackened chicken against the grain.

14. Pour the dressing over the quinoa and salad.

15. Spoon the quinoa salad onto 2 plates and top with the blackened chicken.

Chicken Pozole Stew

2 tablespoons olive oil

1 pound (500 g) chicken wings or bones

Salt

1 ½ pounds (700 g) bone-in chicken thighs, skin removed

6 garlic cloves

1 yellow onion, quartered

1 tablespoon dried oregano

½ teaspoon ground cumin

4 cups (1 liter) chicken stock

1 dried bay leaf

4 to 6 dried guajillo or ancho chiles (depending on your heat preference)

One 28-ounce (822 g) can white hominy, drained and rinsed

1 tablespoon apple cider vinegar

For Serving:

¼ small cabbage, thinly sliced

½ bunch of fresh cilantro/coriander, roughly chopped

1 handful of red radishes, thinly sliced

1 avocado, pitted and sliced

1 lime, halved

1 cup corn chips (optional)

Dollop of plain Greek yogurt (optional)

1. In a deep, heavy-bottomed pot over high heat, heat the olive oil. Add the chicken wings and a large pinch of salt and cook, tossing every so often, until thoroughly browned. Remove from the pan and set aside.

2. Generously season the chicken thighs with salt.

3. Add the chicken thighs to the same pan over high heat, cooking both sides, about 2 minutes per side, until browning. Remove from the pan.

4. Chop 3 of the garlic cloves and leave the remaining 3 whole.

5. In the same pan over high heat, add the onion, chopped garlic, oregano, and cumin. Cook for 3 minutes, until browning.

6. Add the chicken thighs and wings back in and cover with the chicken stock and 1 cup (240 ml) water. Add the bay leaf. Scrape any bits that stick to the bottom of the pan.

7. Bring to a boil, then reduce the heat to medium-low and cook until the chicken thighs are tender, about 45 minutes. Skim any foam or oil off the surface as it cooks.

8. In a small pan, bring water to a boil. Add the chilis, reduce the heat to low, and cook until soft, 10 minutes. Reserve 1 cup of the cooking water. Drain the chilis.

9. In a blender, add the chilis, the remaining garlic, and the reserved cooking water. Blend and set aside.

10. Remove all the meat and the onion quarters from the soup, separating out the thighs from the rest. Pull the meat off the thighs.

11. Pour half of the chili blend into the remaining liquid. Add the hominy and vinegar. Bring to a boil.

12. Taste the broth and if you want more spice, add the remining chili mixture.

13. Return the pulled chicken meat to the soup and cook all together for 10 more minutes.

14. Spoon the soup into 2 bowls and garnish liberally with the cabbage, cilantro, radishes, avocado, lime, and corn chips (if using).

15. Add a dollop of yogurt (if using).

Chopped Salad, Beverly Hills Style

2 large eggs

5 slices/rashers of streaky bacon

One 6-ounce chicken breast (170 g)

2 whole, unpeeled garlic cloves

¼ cup (115 g) balsamic vinegar

1 shallot, diced

½ tablespoon brown sugar

½ teaspoon Dijon mustard

Salt and freshly ground black pepper, to taste

½ cup olive oil

1 large head romaine lettuce, thinly sliced

1 cup (100 g) cherry tomatoes, quartered

1 ripe avocado, pitted and small cubed

1 cup (120 g) small cubes aged cheddar cheese

2 cooked and peeled beets, small cubed

1. Preheat the oven to 400°F (200°C).

2. Boil a small pot of water. Add the eggs and cook for 10 minutes. Remove and drain in a colander, running cold water over them until they are cool enough to touch. Set aside.

3. Line a plate with paper towels.

4. In a large ovenproof frying pan over medium heat, add the bacon. Cook, turning once, until crispy. Keeping the bacon fat in the pan, remove the bacon and drain on the prepared plate.

5. In the same pan over medium-high heat, add the chicken breast. Sear both sides in the bacon fat until browned but not cooked through, 1 minute per side.

6. Add the unpeeled garlic to the pan with the chicken. Transfer to the oven and cook for 10 minutes. Remove and allow to cool.

7. Remove the garlic cloves from their skins and transfer to a cutting board. Crush them with the side of a knife. Add to a small bowl.

8. In the bowl with the garlic, whisk together the balsamic vinegar, shallot, brown sugar, Dijon mustard, salt, and pepper. Slowly drizzle in the olive oil as you whisk, emulsifying slowly until you have a thick, creamy dressing.

9. Peel and cut the hard-boiled eggs into a rough dice.

10. Finely chop the cooked, cooled bacon.

11. Cut the cooked chicken into ½-inch (1-centimeter) cubes.

12. To assemble the salad, layer the shredded lettuce on the bottom of 2 bowls and divide the eggs, bacon, tomatoes, avocado, cheese cubes, and beets between the bowls. Toss with the dressing.

Perfect Paella

2 tablespoons olive oil

1 pound (500 g) chicken wings or bones

Salt

1 ½ pounds (700 g) bone-in chicken thighs, skin removed

6 garlic cloves

1 yellow onion, quartered

1 tablespoon dried oregano

½ teaspoon ground cumin

4 cups (1 liter) chicken stock

1 dried bay leaf

4 to 6 dried guajillo or ancho chiles (depending on your heat preference)

One 28-ounce (822 g) can white hominy, drained and rinsed

1 tablespoon apple cider vinegar

For Serving:

¼ small cabbage, thinly sliced

½ bunch of fresh cilantro/coriander, roughly chopped

1 handful of red radishes, thinly sliced

1 avocado, pitted and sliced

1 lime, halved

1 cup corn chips (optional)

Dollop of plain Greek yogurt (optional)

1. Season the chicken well with salt.

2. Line a plate with paper towels. Set aside.

3. In a medium frying pan with a lid over high heat, add the chorizo. Cook on high until browning. Keeping the grease in the pan, remove the chorizo with a slotted spoon and transfer to the prepared plate.

4. Add the chicken thighs. Sear until browned and released from the pan, about 2 minutes. Flip and cook for another 2 minutes. Remove from the pan.

5. Add oil to the pan if needed and add the onion, bell pepper, and garlic. Reduce the heat slightly and cook until softened, about 5 minutes. Scrape to get any chicken bits off the bottom of the pan.

6. Add the tomatoes, paprika, and saffron and cook on medium-high until the tomatoes are breaking down and the liquid is evaporated, about 5 minutes more.

7. Add the wine and cook until reduced by half. Season with salt if needed.

8. Add the rice, stirring to ensure even coverage. Nestle the chicken thighs and chorizo back in.

9. Evenly pour the broth over the top, ensuring all the rice and chicken is covered. Add the bay leaf.

10. Bring the mixture to a boil, then reduce the heat to medium-low. Stir once after it's boiling to distribute the heat around the pan.

11. Cook for about 20 minutes. Don't stir (this allows a crust to form on the bottom of the pan).

12. Add the shrimp and peas to the top of the mixture. Cook for another 5 minutes. Add a bit of water if your rice isn't cooked through fully.

13. Place a lid or foil over the dish and remove it from the heat, allowing it to steam for 10 minutes.

14. Sprinkle the parsley over the top and serve with lemon wedges!

Chicken Biryani

For the Marinade:

½ cup (37 ml) plain Greek yogurt

¼ cup tomato paste

2 tablespoons olive oil

3 garlic cloves

1-inch piece of fresh ginger

1 teaspoon ground turmeric

1 teaspoon garam marsala

1 teaspoon salt

For the Biryani:

1 pound (400 g) boneless, skin-less chicken thighs

4 tablespoons vegetable oil

2 medium yellow onions, thinly sliced

Salt

2 tablespoons whole milk

1 ½ tablespoons unsalted butter

1 teaspoon saffron threads

5 whole cloves

1 dried bay leaf

1 star anise

3 green cardamon pods

1 cup (225 g) uncooked basmati rice

1 cup fresh cilantro/coriander leaves, roughly chopped

1 cup fresh mint leaves, roughly chopped

½ cup plain Greek yogurt, plus more for serving

1. Make the marinade: In a blender or the bowl of a food processor, add the yogurt, tomato paste, olive oil, garlic, ginger, turmeric, garam marsala, and salt. Blend.

2. Make the biryani: In a large bowl, add the chicken thighs and marinade and toss to coat. Let marinate in the fridge for 30 minutes.

3. Line a plate with paper towels.

4. In a skillet over medium-high heat, heat the vegetable oil and add the onions, sautéing until brown and sweet, 10 minutes. Season with a pinch of salt. Drain onto the prepared plate and set aside.

5. In a saucepot over medium heat, add the milk, butter, and saffron. Cook until the butter has melted, 2 minutes. Remove from the heat and let sit.

6. Bring a large pot of water to a boil and add ½ teaspoon of salt, the cloves, bay leaf, star anise, and cardamom pods. Allow to boil for 5 minutes.

7. Add the rice and allow to boil for 4 minutes. Drain and set aside.

8. Remove the marinated chicken from the fridge. In a heavy-bottomed pot with a lid over medium heat, add the marinated chicken. Cook for 4 minutes, then turn the chicken pieces once. Cover with the lid and cook for another 3 minutes. Turn off the heat.

9. Scatter half of the browned onions all over the chicken. Sprinkle with the cilantro and ½ cup of the mint leaves.

10. Next layer the rice over the mint and cilantro. Drizzle the saffron milk and butter all over the rice.

11. Cover the pot with the lid and cook over low heat, 20 minutes. Remove from the heat and let rest for 5 to 10 minutes. Scatter the remaining onions on top.

12. In a medium bowl, combine the yogurt, the remaining ½ cup mint, and a pinch of salt.

13. Garnish the biryani with a dollop of the yogurt and the mint yogurt sauce.

Warm Steak Salad with Fried Artichokes

For the Pickled Onions:

½ red onion, thinly sliced

¼ cup (60 ml) white wine vinegar

¼ cup (60 ml) water

1 tablespoon sugar

1 teaspoon salt

For the Dressing:

1 tablespoon horseradish (tinned or fresh)

1 tablespoon white wine vinegar

1 tablespoon honey

2 tablespoons olive oil

Salt and freshly ground black pepper, to taste

For the Steak Salad:

One 7-ounce (200-g) filet of beef (you can use sirloin if preferred)

Salt and freshly ground black pepper

12 ounces (350 g) new potatoes, halved and skin on

½ cup (100 ml) sunflower or other high-heat oil

One 7-ounce (200-g) tin oil-packed artichoke hearts, drained

½ cup (40 g) raw walnut halves

2 big handfuls of mixed salad leaves

1 .Make the pickled onions: In a small saucepan, add the vinegar, ¼ cup water, the sugar, and salt. Bring to a boil. Add the onion to a medium bowl and pour over with the vinegar mixture. Let pickle for at least 10 minutes.

2. Make the dressing: In a large bowl, whisk together the horseradish, honey, and white wine vinegar. Add the oil slowly and season with salt and pepper. Set aside.

3. Make the steak salad: Preheat the oven to 375°F (180°C).

4. Remove your steak from the fridge.

5. In a pot, add cold water (enough to cover the potatoes) and salt. Add the potatoes. Bring to a boil. Allow to cook until soft but not falling apart, about 10 minutes. Drain.

6. Line a plate with paper towels. Set aside.

7. In a small saucepan over high heat, heat the sunflower oil. Fry the drained artichokes in the hot oil until crispy. You can tell that they are finished when they start fanning out and air bubbles stop rising to the surface, 6 to 8 minutes. Remove them with a slotted spoon and transfer to the prepared plate. Season them with salt.

8. Season your steak liberally with salt and pepper.

9. In a frying pan over high heat, heat 1 tablespoon oil. Add the steak and fry until you get a nice crispy outer shell on the filet, 2 to 3 minutes per side. Remove and let rest for 5 minutes.

10. Put the walnut halves on a baking sheet and toast in the oven for 5 minutes, or until starting to brown and smell nutty.

11. In the bowl with the dressing, add the potatoes, salad leaves, artichoke hearts, and walnuts and toss. Serve on 2 plates.

12. Slice the steak and top each salad with it. Top with the pickled onions.

APPENDIX II:

Cook Together Conversation Topics

Some prompts to jumpstart the conversation in the kitchen and
around the table.

Conversation Topics

Some prompts to jumpstart the conversation in the kitchen and around the table.

1. If you could only eat one cuisine for the rest of your life, what would it be and why?

2. What's the most adventurous thing you've ever tried cooking at home?

3. If you were a contestant on a cooking show, what dish would win you the competition?

4. What's your go-to comfort food when you're feeling down?

5. If you could have a dinner party with any three people, historical or living, who would they be, and what would you cook for them?

6. What's the strangest food combination you've ever tried that surprisingly tasted amazing?

7. Have you ever had a bad cooking mishap? If so, what happened?

8. If you could travel anywhere in the world just to try one dish, where would you go and what would you eat?

9. What secret ingredient do you add to make a dish extra special?

10. What condiment can you not live without?

11. Are there any foods you can't stand?

12. If you could invent a new kitchen gadget or utensil, what would it do?

13. Share a food memory that brings a smile to your face.

14. What annoys you most in a restaurant?

15. What's the most exotic or unusual ingredient you've ever tasted, and how did it make you feel?

16. If you were to open a restaurant, what would its theme, name and specialty dishes be?

17. Who is the best cook you know?

18. What's your favorite guilty pleasure snack, and do you have any unique ways to enjoy it?

19. What makes a fun dinner party?

20. If you had to create a new holiday centered around food, what would it be called, and what traditions would it involve?

21. Do you have a history of cooking in your family? Have any dishes been passed down through generations?

22. What's your philosophy on sharing food off your plate with others?

23. What is your favorite bagel topping? Pizza topping?

24. What's the most unusual place you've ever eaten a meal, and what did you have?

25. Describe the perfect picnic menu for a romantic date in the park.

26. If you could time-travel to any era in culinary history, when and where would you go, and what would you want to taste?

27. If you could swap lives with a famous chef for a day, who would it be?

28. Describe a food-related challenge or adventure you'd like to embark on in the future (e.g., learning to make sushi from scratch).

29. What's the most unique or bizarre food-related tradition or custom you've encountered in your life?

30. If you had to wear a perfume inspired by your favorite food, what would it smell like?

Acknowledgments

There were many sets of hands that went into the making of this book, and I want to thank everyone who contributed.

Specifically, my number-one partner in the kitchen and out, my husband, James, who keeps the wheels turning in every way imaginable. Little things like helping take on the parenting when I needed time to work and big stuff like constantly pushing me to take this project up again whenever I got worn down. So much wouldn't exist without you. Thank you.

My kids, June and Woody, who inspire me to (attempt to) prove that a mom can do it all. I hope you find something you love in life as much as I love cooking for you.

My family, specifically my parents who grew my interest in food from a young age and later showed me that you can cook these recipes in a kitchen of any size! And my little sister, Alice, who was always up for recipe testing every time the call went out. Sorry about the pork meatballs.

My friends: Kat, who has seen the vision from day one and used all her resources to help me get the word out. Nada, who designed the cover and who always applies her impeccable designs and taste to whatever project I dream up. Lee, who continues to be my number-one recipe fan and whose food styling and artistic sensibility led the photography. Lily, whose love for food re-ignited my passion for this project.

To my incredible photographer, layout designer, and marketing partner Kiyan at Omina JPEG, who made this book what it is. You stuck it out with me for long shoot days, recipe testing and lots and lots of 'what if' brainstorm sessions.

Finally, to Suzy, my editor without whom this book (and I) would be a jumbled mess. I can't thank you enough for taking on this project and making it sing.

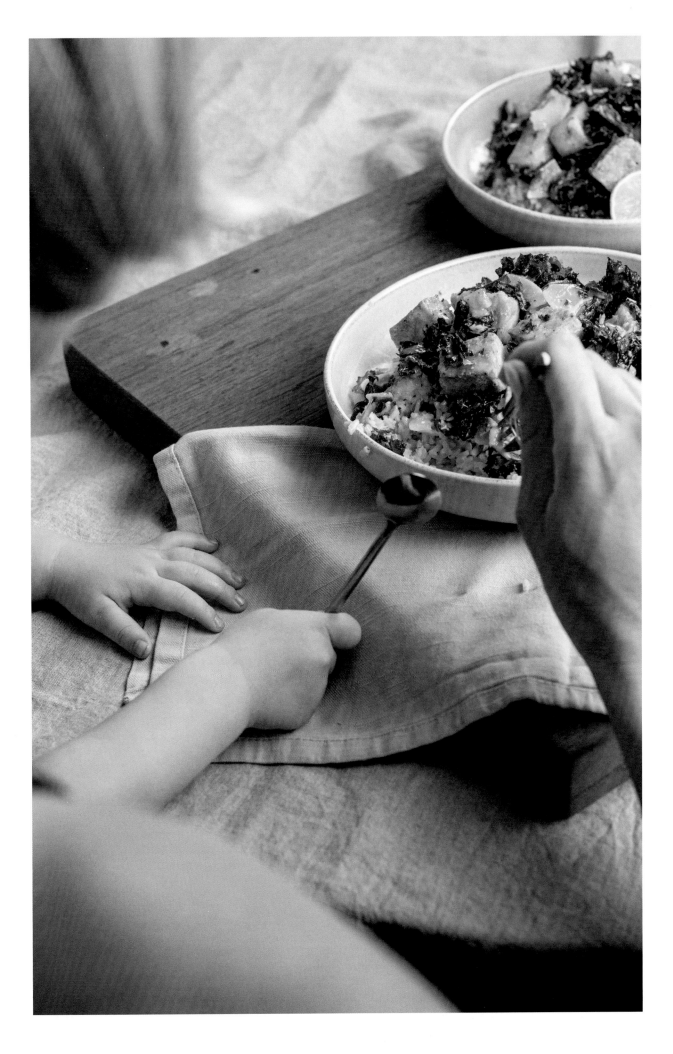

Index

Index

Index

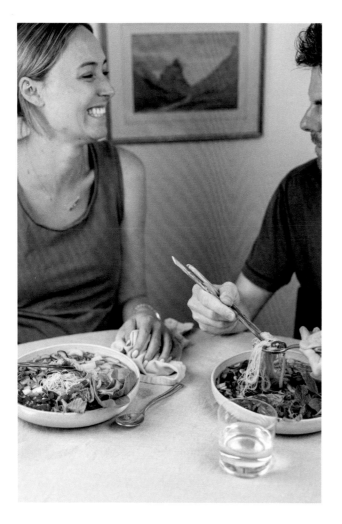

Dorothy Woods is a chef, writer and nutritionist based in the UK, where she lives in Somerset with her family. Her interest in healthy eating began when she was diagnosed with celiac disease aged 14. This really brought home that the way we eat can be harmful to our bodies. But it also taught her that the opposite's true too: the way we eat can also heal our bodies in amazing ways – and when you cook together with the people you love, it can create beautiful bonds between partners and families.

Before turning to teaching and writing she was a private chef for ten years, helping families and individuals overcome diet-related illnesses. She travelled the world with many of her clients, learning about different ingredients and cuisines along the way. She has achieved both a Cuisine Diploma and a Diploma in Gastronomy, Nutrition and Food Trends from Le Cordon Bleu and is a certified Institute for Integrative Nutrition coach.